Souls Visit Me

Maria Simma

Contents

CONTENTS

I bless you Father, Lord of heaven and of earth, for hiding these things from the learned and the clever, and revealing them to mere children. Yes, Father, for that is what it pleased you to do.

Mt. 11:25–26

Take yourselves for instance, brothers, at the time when you were called: How many of you were wise in the ordinary sense of the word, how many were influential people, or came from noble families? No, it was to shame the wise that God chose what is foolish by human reckoning, and to shame what is strong that he chose what is weak by human reckoning; those whom the world thinks common and contemptible are the ones that God has chosen—those who are nothing at all to show up those who are everything. The human race has nothing to boast about to God.

1 Cor., 1:26–29

There is a purgatory, and the souls retained there are being helped through the intercession of the faithful.

Council of Trent

Foreword

Spiritus ubi vult spirat
The Spirit breathes where he wills . . .

The book, *Meine Erlebnisse mit Armen Seelen*, by Maria
Simma, has been attacked, in a manner not to the point, in
several newspapers. This compels me as the publisher to express my viewpoint:

Before I decided to publish the book, I wanted to carefully
examine everything. I went to the hometown of Maria Simma,
to Sonntag in the Grossen Walsertal, where I had a lengthy talk
with her spiritual director, Pastor Alfons Matt. The latter also
empowered me to print in this book, in an abbreviated form,
his report on Maria Simma to the competent bishop. We were
permitted to have made for the archives of our publishing
house photocopies of a six-page psychological test given by
Dr. Ewald Böhm at the request of a professor of theology in
Innsbruck. It is important to know that according to this report
there can be no question of hysteria and psychopathy. In the

village of Sonntag I also made inquiries with neighbors and visited the new shrine for pilgrims.

To express it briefly, I am concerned only about the right answer to the question: Is Maria Simma authentic or not? If the facts described in this book are genuine, then I see therein, so to speak, divine credentials for the supernaturalness of her charisma. That it is, therefore, more than telepathy, for instance, and that her experiences are credible.

Possibility of a Control

In the report given by Pastor Alfons Matt, we read on page 17, "A certain control can be exercised if one checks the messages which Maria Simma had to send in regard to certain Poor Souls to their relatives, for most of those cases were entirely unknown to her." (In the report by Father Matt to Auxiliary Bishop Tschann in Feldkirch there follows here a list of names of deceased persons and their petitions. "Most of the messages I sent to the various parish rectories for investigation and for forwarding, adding the petition to be passed on in case the facts were found to be correct. In the cases where I underlined the words, I received an answer in return saying that they were correct.")

I now ask any likely critics to abstain from any speculations and unfavorable comments and be satisfied, for the time being, with the proof of the genuineness or fraudulency of the case, and that on the basis of the facts described in the book. Everything will follow of itself.

I publicly declare herewith that I shall immediately withdraw the book from distribution if sound proof can be offered that Maria Simma and her spiritual director were guilty of fraud and that the facts described in the book are simulated even though there are hundreds of witnesses in dozens of towns.

From the very beginning we have deliberately spoken plainly. We gave the name, hometown, personal records and photo of Maria Simma so that anyone who, with an honest intention, wishes to investigate the case can do so (just as at the International Office of Physicians in Lourdes, anyone can research the scientifically inexplicable miracles). To critics who are in earnest, this publishing house is also willing to submit other statements and documents as far as they are in my possession.

The book by Maria Simma was not written for the satisfaction of sensational curiosity but rather for edification, to confront the reader with the fact of a purgatory and to remind him to pray for the dead.

What Does Vatican II Say About Private Revelations?

If God gives a charism, then, in my opinion, it is certainly not for private amusement. Brother Claus von der Flüe had a vision of the Most Blessed Trinity surely not just for his own personal edification, and a Jeanne d'Arc of Lorraine heard voices not simply for private enjoyment but rather for the deliverance of an entire country.

No Catholic is obliged to believe in private revelations but it is an undeniable fact that there have been and still are in the Church countless private revelations. Since Francis of Assisi, for instance, there have been over 300 cases of stigmatization which have been verified. Many things in the Church can be traced to private revelations: the processions on the Feast of

Corpus Christi, devotion to the Most Sacred Heart, the rosary, Lourdes, etc. We need not be ashamed of this. Wouldn't we have God distribute also in our days any of the charismatic gifts about which St. Paul speaks so clearly?

Concerning these gifts, Vatican Council II wrote: "These charismatic gifts, whether they be the most outstanding or the most simple and widely diffused, are to be received with thanksgiving and consolation, for they are exceedingly suitable and useful for the needs of the Church. Still, extraordinary gifts are not to be rashly sought after, nor are the fruits of apostolic labor to be presumptiously expected from them. In any case, judgment as to their genuineness and proper use belongs to those who preside over the Church and to whose special competence it belongs, not indeed to extinguish the Spirit, but to test all things and hold fast to that which is good." ("Constitution on the Church," #12)

Alfons Matt writes on page 18: "Whatever Maria Simma has learned from the Poor Souls concerning the present time, its troubles, dangers and remedies, and what she herself was given to see in her hours of frightening sufferings for her own information and consolation perfectly agrees with the doctrine on God's justice and love as well as with that of purgatory and of the judgment and the experiences of the ecclesiastical experiences." Why, therefore, all this sensitivity when apparitions of the Poor Souls is not new in the Church. (There exists abundant literature on this subject even from our present time.) Even St. John Bosco of Turin (1815–1888) had an apparition of a deceased friend, witnessed by 20 other seminarians, which made a terrifying and indelible impression on all of them. Also, famous St. Margaret Mary Alacoque, in her autobiography, tells us of an apparition of a Benedictine monk. The New Testament explicitly testifies to the fact that the souls of deceased persons can appear to the living; thus Mt. 27:52−54 describes how, "after Christ's resurrection, departed souls appeared to many persons."

The Key Person

In a document of the Chancery Office at Feldkirch, it says, concerning Father Alfons Matt, "The pastor himself is a completely integrated person and a priest who shows no trace of a visionary. He is a venerable Priest of 77 years."

My own entirely personal opinion is this: Suppose Maria Simma is authentic, why then doesn't one believe Alfons Matt who is said to be an ideal priest of great integrity and in the Simma case certainly the main witness and key figure?

Suppose Maria Simma is not authentic. Then Alfons Matt would have become the victim of a deceiver; though having known her for decades, he would be lacking the gift of discernment of spirits. In such a case would he be considered a well integrated and ideal priest? No one will expect the Bishop of Feldkirch to publicly approve Maria Simma as long as she is living; that would contradict all ecclesiastical praxis which, in cases where there is no obvious fraud, follows the counsel of Gamaliel (Acts 5:34−40).

The humility and poverty of Maria Simma are for us the best guarantee for her genuineness; had she been proud and conceited we wouldn't have raised a finger in her behalf. But this is just where some take scandal; the Jews, too, were scandalized seeing Jesus converse with simple ignorant fishermen, publicans and sinners. Many modern Catholics consider themselves so enlightened that they can't understand why Our Lady appeared in Lourdes and Fatima to such simple shepherd children. Many even reject Fatima in spite of the miracle of the sun, witnessed in 1917 by 70,000 persons and on which the entire world press reported.

God's Handwriting

God loves to choose the weak in order to confound the strong. It is in a weak instrument that the greatness of His power becomes manifest. Had David been equal to Goliath as a warrior, no one would have believed in divine intervention.

With unheard of perception St. Paul discerned the hidden reasons when he writes in his first letter to the Corinthians, "If it was God's wisdom that human wisdom should not know God, it was because God wanted to save those who have faith through the foolishness of the message that we preach (I Cor. 19–20).

How stupid is that saying about "peripheral" things (Mary, the saints, etc.). As though the periphery does not belong to the whole! What, for instance, would Europe be without marginal states? Today many Catholics are infected by modernistic ideas and think they can throw overboard anything that has to do with charism and mysticism.

Why do our great airlines solicit passengers by means of giant posters, "Fly to India to Meditate!" Why do hundreds of thousands of hippies populate the banks of the Ganges? Because modern man also hungers for mysticism. However, under the trend of progressive ideas, faith is so badly rationalized that there is no longer place for mysticism (derived from the Greek "mysterium"—secret).

In closing I want to bring to mind the words of Karl Rahner, theologian of Vatican II: "Private revelations are not a luxury for the Church but are essentially directives on how the Church should act in a certain situation concerning salvation.'' In any case, we have acted in good faith and shall submit ourselves to the truth. As long, however, as we act in good faith we enjoy protection by the law of tolerance and have the right to an objective and fair critique.

ARNOLD GUILLET

An Abridged Report on Maria Simma

written by Pastor Alfons Matt, and submitted to the Ordinary of the Diocese, bishop Franz Tschann, Auxiliary Bishop of Feldkirch, +1955

"I see these souls in the sufferings of purgatory and discern two effects: The first one is that they bear these sufferings willingly and that they believe, when considering their guilt and God's infinite greatness, that God has exercised great mercy in their regard...
The other effect is the joy they experience when considering the disposition God made in their regard, who acted only with the greatest love and mercy toward them."

St. Catherine of Genoa, "Treatise on Purgatory," Chapter 16

Family and Life of Maria Simma

Maria Agatha Simma was born in Sonntag/Vorarlberg, February 5, 1915, as the second child of Joseph Anton Simma and Aloysia Rinderer. Sonntag is located far back in the Grossen Walsertal, about 30 km east of Feldkirch. Her father, Joseph Anton Simma, was a son of the owner of the Löwen Inn, also named Joseph Anton, and of Anna Pfisterer of Sonntag. He earned his living as a dairy man and, later, for years, as a farmhand for his brother, Johann Simma, a farmer in Bregenz. There he became acquainted with Aloysia Rinderer, daughter of a railroader, who had been adopted by his brother Johann. In spite of the 18 years difference in their ages, eventually they were married. Both were poor when entering marriage. They moved into a house in Sonntag-Litze. During World War I, Maria's father served as a mailman; later on as a roadmaker and a day laborer, and finally he retired. He moved with his wife and eight children into an old house which he had inherited from a good old man, Franz Bickel, a carpenter. Because of the family's poverty, the children were, at an early age, sent to earn their living as temporary laborers and housemaids.

From early youth Maria was deeply religious and zealously attended the religious instruction given by Pastor Dr. Karl Fritz. After her graduation from grammar school she came to Swabia, and later to Hard, Nenzing, and Lauterbach. She had a great desire to enter the convent but three times she had to leave on account of her frail constitution. She obtained her outfit for the convent partly by begging, partly by her work. For three years she served as a maid in St. Joseph Home, Feldkirch. After leaving the convent in Gaissau, Maria kept house for her father and took care of the cleaning of the church. Since the death of her father, in 1947, she has been living alone in the parental home. In order to increase her meager income, she does some gardening on a small scale. Naturally, she is living in very poor circumstances and is therefore dependent on some help by good people.

Maria's stay in a convent at three different times was religiously of a great advantage to her and a preparation for her calling to an apostolate for the Poor Souls. Her religious life is characterized by a childlike love of Mary, the desire to help the Suffering Souls and to support the missions in pagan lands. She vowed virginity in honor of Mary and made the act of total consecration to Jesus through Mary according to St. Louis M. Grignion de Montfort, especially for the Poor Souls, and also offered herself to Jesus as a victim of love and reparation. Maria Simma finally seems to have found her God-given vocation—to help the Poor Souls through prayer, atoning suffering, and an active apostolate. At the time of the Nazi regime, and ever since then, she has helped to prepare the children for their First Confession and Communion; also on other occasions she gives supplementary religious instructions for which she has shown special talent and skill.

4

Help for the Poor Souls

Since childhood Maria Simma has helped the Poor Souls through prayer and application of indulgences. Since 1940, Poor Souls came to her now and then asking for prayer. On All Saints' Day, 1953, she started her help by expiatory suffering for the Poor Souls.

Maria had to take upon herself severe sufferings for an officer who had died in Kärnten in 1660. The kind of suffering corresponded to the kind of sins committed. She was told that in the week of Poor Souls' Day the souls in purgatory receive special privileges through Mary's great mercy. She also learned that the month of November is a time of special graces for them.

Maria was happy when the month of November came to an end, but her sufferings started again and were even worse on the Feast of the Immaculate Conception. A priest from Cologne, of the year 555, appeared and made a desperate impression. He said he needed expiatory sufferings but Maria would have to take them upon herself absolutely voluntarily, otherwise he would have to suffer to the end of the world. She accepted and, thereupon, followed a week of severe sufferings. The soul came every night and laid new sufferings upon her. It was as though someone would tear all her limbs apart. With a heavy pressure the soul laid himself on Maria and again and again sharp daggers were thrust violently into her body from all sides. At another time it was as though a blunt piece of iron were thrust into her body, striking some obstacle, splitting, and then distributing itself into all parts of the body. This soul had to do penance for the murders of the companions of St.

Ursula, for his apostasy, for repeated adultery and for sacriligious celebration of the Eucharistic Sacrifice.

Again and again more souls were coming, asking for help. The atoning sufferings for abortion and sins against chastity consisted in fearful spasms and nausea. Then again it seemed to her that she was lying for hours between blocks of ice, the cold penetrating to her very marrow. It was atoning suffering for lukewarmness and religious coldness. After the above mentioned severe case concerning the priest from Cologne, she was told that she would still have to take over six other souls who could be released only by voluntary atoning suffering. Later she would be able to release many souls through the mercy of the Mother of Jesus.

During the first six months the following souls came to her: a certain Berta from France who died in 1740, a woman from Vienna who died in 1810, a prostitute from Italy, two unmarried women from Innsbruck who had died in a plane crash, and an Italian priest. There also came others who could be helped by lighter sufferings and prayer.

Maria Simma took upon herself all those sacrifices no matter how difficult it was at times. Yes, naturally, often she would not have been able to endure it.

In August 1954, a new way of helping the Poor Souls began. A certain Paul Gisinger of Koblach came with the petition that his seven children (he mentioned them by name) donate 100 shillings for the World Mission and have two Holy Masses offered; then he would be released. In October, Maria received about 42 more such petitions for smaller or larger contributions for the World Mission, for Mass stipends, and petitions for the praying of the rosary. All of these souls came personally and of their own accord without Maria Simma's having inquired about them.

6

Also in October 1954, a Poor Soul told Maria Simma that in the week of Poor Souls' Day she herself could inquire about those souls whose relatives were willing to help them by fulfilling what would be requested. Before this she had asked several times about certain Poor Souls and had sometimes received an answer. She was permitted to accept such inquiries until November 20, and was told she would still receive answers concerning these souls during the Marian Year. In October and November, and until the Feast of the Immaculate Conception every night Poor Souls came for whom she had to pray and at times to suffer. In the beginning she had to say all the required prayers herself. When the requests became too numerous, she was permitted to ask people for help who were willing to comply conscientiously with the requests. If it was the soul of a priest who asked for help, the request for prayers had to be fulfilled by a priest. After the close of the Holy Year, Maria Simma was given a few days rest, but then again souls came for whom Maria of her own free will and according to her own judgment could and would take sufferings upon herself.

How Do the Poor Souls Appear?

. . . . in diverse shapes and manners. Some announce themselves by knocking; others are suddenly there. Some appear in human form, visible and clear as in life, usually in their weekday clothes; others appear hazy and indistinct; Poor Souls who are suffering a specially painful purgation make a desperate impression.

The more they are being cleansed by atoning sufferings, the clearer and friendlier they become. Frequently they report in what manner they have failed and how through God's mercy

7

they have escaped the pains of hell. Often, they add instructions and admonitions.

With some other souls, Maria just senses their presence and becomes cognizant that she is to pray and suffer for them. During Lent, Poor Souls make their presence known only by sufferings which she has to bear during the night or at times also during the day.

It also happens that Poor Souls appear in atrocious, frightening shapes. At times they talk the way they spoke during life, in their dialect. Those of a foreign language speak in broken German and with a foreign accent, i.e., in a very individualistic manner.

Estimation of the Apparitions

Are they reality or imagination, fancies that have been brought about in an artificial way, by desire or reading? There are diverse facts which attest to the reality of the apparitions and atoning sufferings.

1. It is true that Maria Simma had the desire to help the Poor Souls from earliest childhood, and she zealously made use of any days on which one could gain special indulgences; she also said many indulgeneed prayers for the Poor Souls. However, that one could help the Suffering Souls also by atoning suffering, she did not know until it came over her.

These atoning sufferings are as painful as purgatory, and it required a heroic spirit of sacrifice and the realization of her vow in favor of the Poor Souls to take upon herself absolutely of her own free will these atoning sufferings.

One day she uttered the desire that the Poor Souls come

less frequently so that she would have the necessary sleep; otherwise she would no longer be able to do her work. The answer was: Hadn't she by vow offered herself as a victim soul? Was that perhaps only for show and pious imagination? She would have to accept if the Blessed Mother held her to her word. Moreover, she should cook better and eat better, then she would also be able to stand more. Human beings could endure more than they think possible. Besides, she shouldn't forget that the Poor Souls would help her to do her day's work.

Maria Simma distinguishes clearly between what is happening to her in a dream and what in a waking state. The Poor Souls wake her up, address her and come over her with their sufferings. Often she also had to take sufferings during her daily duties and functions. A proof that this is not a question of ordinary sickness lies in the fact that part of these sufferings were announced beforehand and that they suddenly stopped after the number of hours announced were over. Maria Simma frequently declared to me how much she desired that the Marian Year would come to an end, so heavily everything was pressing on her. The Poor Souls repeatedly reprimanded her for such desires, telling her she should take everything upon herself the way God sent it.

2. Frequently the wish has been expressed that Maria Simma should be observed unseen during the night in order to find out the truth of the matter. Some young men have done that out of their own curiosity because they thought the whole affair was nothing but a fraud. They were F.N., A.N., W.P., E.B., W.B., and, in some degree, also the girl, K.B. During two nights before the Feast of the Immaculate Conception, in 1954, they climbed on a ladder to the flower box before Maria's bedroom window, which was open. There they heard

Maria moan and weep: they saw how she was searching for her handkerchief to dry her tears. They heard how she was talking with the Poor Souls, was asking questions, and observed her taking notes. They saw and heard nothing of the Poor Souls. From then on they no longer derided and ridiculed the apparitions of the Poor Souls. It made them thoughtful. The oldest of these young men told me about what he had observed and how it had impressed him. Maria Simma herself learned from one of the Poor Souls that someone had observed her during two nights and that it had been for the good of the listeners. When she learned that the boys had neither seen nor heard the Poor Souls, she asked one of the latter for an explanation.

Answer: "Those boys are still alive."

Maria: "But I too am still alive and yet I hear you."

Answer: "You belong to us. We are in darkness. The way to you is bright."

Maria: "But if I would not accept you?"

Soul: "Through the Mercy of God we may force you because you belong to us."

Maria: "What does that mean, 'You belong to us'?"

Soul: "Through your vow you surrendered yourself in a special way to the Mother of Mercy; she handed you over to us; therefore, the way to you is clear for many souls. You do well to accept us willingly out of charity and compassion. In this way you can release us quicker; you will suffer less; will receive more graces and earn more merits, and you will also learn more concerning the souls about whom you are inquiring."

3. A certain control can be exercised by checking the messages which Maria Simma had to send in behalf of Poor Souls to their relatives, for most of the cases were entirely unknown to her. (In this report to Auxiliary Bishop Tschann there follows a long list of names of deceased persons and their requests.) Most of the messages, Father Matt continues, I handed on to the respective parish rectories to be checked and the petitions for forwarding in case the statements correspond with the truth. I underlined the cases in which I received an answer stating that everything was correct.

4. From reports of the Poor Souls for which Maria Simma had to do atoning suffering, I could gather various circumstances of which, on account of her degree of culture, Maria Simma couldn't know, as for instance in regard to that priest from Cologne who helped in the massacre of St. Ursula and her companions.

At the time of the avalanche catastrophe in January 1954, Maria Simma was told by the Poor Souls that there were victims buried under the snow who were still alive. The last living victim was found two days later in Blons. Other catastrophies that occurred during the Marian Year were also foretold to her. In the summer of 1954, two days before the newspapers wrote about it, she told me of the great flood. The Poor Souls had spoken to her about it.

5. Subjectively, Maria Simma is sincere and not restrained. Since the beginning of her atoning sufferings, she makes a calmer and more well-balanced impression than before. At the end of the Marian Year the strain during the last months before the Feast of the Immaculate Conception showed itself in great need of sleep, as it would with any normal human being.

6. Whatever Maria Simma learned from the Poor Souls

11

concerning our present times, its troubles, dangers and remedies, and what, in hours of greatest sufferings she had been shown for better understanding and consolation, is in perfect harmony with the doctrine on God's justice and mercy as well as the doctrine on purgatory and with the knowledge and the experiences of ecclesiastical authority.

7. There have been misgivings concerning the fact that Maria Simma can ask the Poor Souls questions and receives appropriate answers from them. One rightly fears that this will be exploited by curious people for sensational purposes.

At first a few persons begged Maria Simma to inquire about something concerning close relatives. In the middle of October it was made known to her that during the week after All Souls' Day she could inquire about any soul whose relatives would accept and perform the works that soul would need for its release. No doubt it pleases God when relatives are concerned about their deceased.

She was also told that there are Poor Souls for whom she is not *obliged* to perform the necessary works but she *may* do so. Usually, in such cases, there was question of souls in the lowest stage in purgatory. Through the special mercy of the Mother of Mercy they were permitted to ask for release. Literally she was told: "They have to tell you that you are not *obliged* to accept them, but that you *may* accept them. Yes, in regard to some, you even must pray to be able to accept them. If you refuse such souls you do not become guilty. Also, these souls may not disturb you for a second time. However, if you willingly accept them, you will also receive greater graces. By that we then shall be able to give you more information about the deceased."

Therefore there is here no question of sensation but of obtaining grace for the suffering souls. Only when people asked from sheer curiosity, as some had wanted to do concerning Hitler and Stalin, did she receive either no answer at all or was refused.

In November 1954, it became gradually known that one could ask questions. However, many questions, coming from a great distance, arrived when the designated time was over.

Not always and everywhere was the necessary discretion observed so that the respective cases were gossiped about. Truthful and false assertions were passed on to others. There were two cases especially which were talked about and caused some scandal: An innkeeper in S. had died suddenly in October 1954. He hadn't been a zealous churchgoer nor had he been especially active in his religion. When Maria Simma received an inquiry in his regard, she was told that the Masses one would have offered for him wouldn't help him much because he had been indifferent as to attending Mass. Later on, Maria Simma again received some answer in his regard, namely, that he would be released if one would give 3,000 shillings. The brother of the deceased and the former's wife prayed much that he would still be released during the Marian Year. They also gave the above mentioned sum for the missions. Soon after, the soul was released from purgatory and that was because he had often defended in conversation the Catholic faith, and the virginity of the Blessed Mother. Because the circumstances of this case were not all known to the people, some, hearing of the soul's release, were scandalized and expressed the opinion that purgatory wasn't so severe.

The second case, too, shows how God, at times, even in such matters, allows human weakness to creep in, partly as a trial, partly as a warning. This case has to do with the steward at a Sisters' convent in B., who had been killed in a traffic accident. The Sisters at that convent had someone inquire with Maria Simma about him. She answered that he had been released from purgatory. However, when later on she once more looked up the slip on which, during the night she had jotted down the various answers, she noticed her mistake, for there it was written that he could not yet be released.

In the meantime, the first answer had been spread abroad in B. causing a big uproar because the steward had been in bad repute. Maria asked one of the Poor Souls whether it had been her fault that, in copying and handing on the answer the first time, the "not" had been overlooked. The answer was, "On the one hand, you, too, are to blame because you acted too hastily. But then the devil had a share in it too. However, the whole affair had some good effects too. People should know that discretion in such matters is simply a must. That's why God permitted it. Besides, it was a humiliation for you, and that was good. You are not to know for how long you may expect answers to your inquiries. That depends on the inquirers, whether they can be discreet or not. It is much more meritorious to assume the sponsorship for a soul, i.e., the willingness to release some unknown soul who has a certain baptismal name one mentions, and to make for it the sacrifices needed for its release."

On the Feast of the Presentation of Our Lord in the Temple, February 2, Maria Simma no longer received as many answers to inquiries that were made, and then only each time the answers came for a number of souls together, so that one didn't know what each individual soul in the group really needed. This was necessary, she was told, in order to counteract curiosity, the result being that fewer inquiries would be made and sensationalism would be restrained. One should by proper discretion protect this modest source of help for the Poor Souls from drying up as long as the Mother of Our Lord wished to apply it to some Poor Souls.

Intrigues of the Devil

Just as the devil, in the case of the above mentioned steward of a convent who was killed in an accident, caused great confusion, so he also came frequently to Maria Simma to frighten her and divert her from her work of atonement. Sometimes he appeared as an angel of light, once in the form of Pastor Reisch von Nerrzing, who for a time had been her confessor; then again as Canon Sattler, chaplain at St. Joseph's Institute, and again as Sister Superior of the Sacred Heart Sisters in Hall, in the Tirol. Canon Sattler was almost canonizing Maria, to make her proud.

Pastor Reisch von Nerrzing and the superior of Hall tried to persuade her to withdraw her vow of total consecration to Mary according to St. Louis M. de Grignion de Montfort. From this she recognized that she was dealing with Satan in disguise and she chased him off with the words, "If you are the devil, I command you in the name of Jesus to leave me." She sprinkled Holy Water—and everything disappeared.

It was especially harrassing in Holy Week of 1954. The Blessed Mother had told her beforehand that during that week great trials and sacrifices would await her, and she would have to suffer them alone. About this Maria Simma jotted down the following: "From April 10–17, 1954, the devil had almost complete control over me. It seemed to me that I was rather in hell than on earth. As a reason, the devil alleged that I had often confessed and communicated unworthily and that once I had committed a serious sin and had lightly passed it over. I answered, 'I know nothing about that.' Thereupon his answer was, 'That is because your conscience has already become so dormant that you are now entirely in my power. These apparitions of Poor Souls are deceptions caused by us. None of these souls has been released. We told you this time and again. In your stupidity you didn't notice it. Now you must bitterly feel that it is so.' And he added that, because I was thrown into hell through my stupidity, he wouldn't be too hard on me and wouldn't give me the worst place in hell. In short, I thought from all this that I was in hell."

Now and then the devil made a terrible uproar as if the whole house would collapse or was ablaze. Or again a flame would suddenly flare up in the room, or it seemed a shot was suddenly fired right before Maria Simma's bed. A Poor Soul consoled her, "Do not be surprized that you have to suffer also from the evil one. The temptor is allowed to torment souls in purgatory also, and even cruelly, in order to purify them. It is done not out of wrath but out of mercy, for these souls are vessels of mercy, destined for eternal glory. I warn you, Satan is most enraged about you. He wants to throw you into confusion wherever he can. Could he torment you as he would like to, he would tear you into small pieces. You would not be able to receive or read any literature the contents of which is a help for the souls in purgatory. He can harm you only so much as God permits because you are under the special protection of the Mother of God, and the devil fears her as one fears death by the sword. He is looking for every opportunity to take revenge on you. He even wants to get you so confused that you will take back your vow of dedication to the Blessed Mother, thus breaking off communication with the Poor Souls. I warn you, with such tricks he has already succeeded with other souls, some of whom he has even thrown into hell. Especially those lost souls would be glad to get you where they are themselves. Fear not; be humble! The more unassuming you are, the less power the hellish fiend will have over you; moreover, we are there to help you, but above all the Mother of Mercy will assist you."

Maria reports: "From 9:00 P.M. on December 2, 1954, until 4:30 A.M. the following day, I suffered as if from glowing flames. Not a Poor Soul was to be seen. I was in great desolation. Now and then I heard a hellish uproar and was seized by a great fear. Then a hellish voice screamed, 'Soon we shall come to get you, you stupid thing!' It was terrifying, almost enough to drive me to despair. The worst thing was that I felt also forsaken by God. I could not pray, and I felt as a prey of the devil. Early the following morning, at 4:30 A.M., the torture and the horrible fear of hell suddenly ceased."

Attitude of the Population

When Maria's experiences with the Poor Souls became known, there was great excitement among the people. This was something new, strange. One could hear people say that never yet had a person come back from the other world. Some believed spontaneously; others were more cautious. Again, others rejected everything. Many wanted to have information about their deceased relatives and, therefore, gave much help to the Poor Souls. They still continue to do so with great zeal, saying one should help if one can do so; the Poor Souls need it. After their own death, they, too, would be happy if others would then help them, and if they themselves should provide this kind of help beforehand. Others are made to realize that there is an eternity; they are aroused from their lethargy and become uncertain. Again others say that, if it wouldn't be Maria Simma, they might believe. In their eyes she is too simple, too poor, too little esteemed.

Why Donations?

Now and then people became disconcerted because the Poor Souls requested donations for the World Missions and Mass stipends in their behalf. Maria Simma did not accept any money for such purposes; people had to take it to the rectory.

The reason for helping certain poor souls also by financial sacrifices is that, by contributions toward some good purposes, they can receive great relief. Maria was told that, at present, support of the missions was an especially good work because the needs in mission countries were so great and with adequate help the harvest would be abundant, especially in Africa and South America. Everyone, she was told, has the obligation to support the missions and some had neglected this duty during their lifetime. Moreover, many a Poor Soul had still to make up for unpaid debts or for an unjust Last Will, or any other injustice for which he had not yet atoned.

If now and then persons make Maria Simma a present or a financial donation for postage, one cannot label that as wrong. She, on her part, does not ask for anything and does everything gratis. She in her great poverty certainly may accept an alms, as the help she gives to the Poor Souls makes great demands upon her time.

Visions of Purgatory

In answer to a question, Maria Simma once answered, "Purgatory is in many places. Souls do not come from purgatory but with purgatory." Repeatedly, she has seen purgatory—sections of it, now this, now that.

There are a great number of souls in purgatory. There is a steady coming and going. Once she saw a great crowd of souls, all unknown to her. The souls who had sinned against faith had a dark flame over their hearts; others, who had sinned against chastity, a red flame.

At other times, she saw the Poor Souls in certain groups: priests, religious men, religious women, or groups of Catholics, Protestants, pagans. Souls of Catholics have to endure greater sufferings than those of Protestants. Pagans, on the other hand, have a still lighter purgatory, but they receive less help and have to suffer longer. Catholics receive more help and are released quicker.

She also saw many religious, men and women, suffering in purgatory on account of lukewarmness and uncharitableness. Even six-year-old children may be in purgatory for quite some time. In purgatory there was revealed to Maria the marvellous harmony between the love and justice of God. Every soul is punished according to the kind of its failings and its mental state at the time the sin was committed.

The severity of the sufferings shows great differences. Some souls suffer as one does here on earth in a laborious life and have to wait for the vision of God. One day of a severe purgatory is harder than ten years of a lighter purgatory. Duration shows up great differences. The priest from Cologne was in purgatory from the year 555 until Ascension Day, 1954. Had he not been released by the atoning sufferings of Maria Simma, he would have remained in horrible sufferings for a long time. There are souls who will have to bear severe sufferings until the end of time. Others have to suffer for only half an hour or even less; they fly, as it were, through purgatory.

The devil may torture Poor Souls, especially those through whose fault others had been condemned to hell.

The Poor Souls bear their sufferings with marvellous patience, praising the mercy of God, thanks to which they escaped hell. They know that they deserve their sufferings and they repent of their failings. They implore the help of Mary, Mother of Mercy. Maria Simma saw many souls waiting for the help of the Blessed Mother.

Whoever in this life thinks that purgatory is harmless and of no account will have to pay for it severely.

How Can We Help the Poor Souls?

1. Above all by the Holy Sacrifice of the Mass; nothing can take its place.
2. Atoning suffering, physical or spiritual, offered for the Poor Souls obtains great relief for them.
3. Next to the Eucharistic Sacrifice, the rosary is the most efficacious means in helping the Poor Souls. Daily, through the rosary, numerous souls are released who otherwise would have to suffer for many more years.
4. The devotion of the Holy Way of the Cross can also bring great relief.
5. As the Poor Souls tell us, indulgences are invaluable. They are the application of the satisfaction rendered through Jesus Christ to the Heavenly Father. Whoever during life is

eager to apply indulgences to the Poor Souls will, more than others, receive the graces to gain perfectly that special indulgence at the hour of death. It is cruel not to use these treasures of the Church for the Poor Souls. Is it not a cruelty if, standing before a mountain of gold pieces and having the possibility to distribute therefrom as much as you wish to a person in dire need who himself is not able to obtain some, you, yourself, do not bother to stretch out your hand to give? In some places zeal for indulgenced prayers is dwindling year after year as it is here in my Switzerland. People should be more encouraged to pursue this practice.

6. Almsgiving and other good works, especially donations for World Missions.

7. Burning of candles helps the Poor Souls. First, because it is an act of thoughtfulness and charity, and, second, because the candles have been blessed and illuminate the darkness of the Poor Souls.

The soul of an eleven year old child of the Kaiser family asked Maria Simma for prayers. It is suffering in purgatory because on All Souls' Day it had extinguished the little lights at the cemetery and had stolen the wax to play with. She had been told that blessed candles are of great value for the Poor Souls. Once, on Candlemas, Maria had to light two candles for a Poor Soul during the time she was bearing atoning sufferings for that soul.

8. The sprinkling of Holy Water also alleviates the pain. One day when Maria was going out and sprinkled some Holy Water for the Poor Souls, a voice was heard saying, "More!"

All these comforting means do not help all in equal measure.

Those who did not value Holy Mass enough during life will not find the Mass efficacious for them in purgatory either. Whoever was hardhearted in life receives little help. Those who sinned through calumny have to undergo great sufferings. Souls who had a receptive heart in life receive much help. One soul who had been negligent in attending Mass was allowed to ask for eight Masses because, when alive, she had once had eight Masses offered for a Poor Soul.

Mary and the Poor Souls

Mary is for the Poor Souls the Mother of Mercy. Maria Simma was told that when her holy name resounds through purgatory the suffering souls feel a great joy. On the Feast of the Assumption, a poor soul said that Mary, at her death, had asked Jesus that all souls who at that time were in purgatory would be released, and that Christ had granted this petition to His Mother. These souls had then accompanied Mary into heaven because on that day she was crowned Mother of Mercy and Mother of Divine Grace. Mary distributes graces in purgatory according to God's holy will; she often goes through purgatory. This is how Maria Simma saw it.

The Poor Souls and the Dying

During the night before All Saint's Day, a soul said, "Today on this All Saints' Day two people will die in Vorarlberg, two people who are in great danger of being eternally lost. They can be saved only if one ardently prays for them." This is what Maria Simma did, supported by others. The following night a soul came and said that the two escaped hell and were now in purgatory. The one sick man had, at the end, asked for the last Sacraments; the other had refused them.

The Poor Souls say that many go to hell because we do not pray enough for them. One should pray morning and night the indulgenced prayer: "O, Jesus, lover of souls, I pray and beseech Thee, by the agony of Thy Most Sacred Heart and by the sorrows of Thy Holy Mother, cleanse in Thy Blood the sinners of the whole world who are now in their agony and are to die this day (night)." "Sacred Heart of Jesus, once in agony, have pity on the dying. Amen."

Maria Simma once saw many souls who were on a scale between hell and purgatory.

Instructions

The Poor Souls are very much concerned about us human beings and the Kingdom of God. We can conclude this from certain instructions they gave Maria Simma. Here follow some of those she had noted:

One should not complain about today's evil times.

Parents cannot render a child a worse service than by complying to its every wish and giving it whatever it wants, if only it is satisfied and doesn't scream. In this way haughtiness is planted in the child's heart. One should tell parents that they, in the first place, are to be blamed for this.

The child comes to school and cannot even pray the Our Father; yes, cannot even make the Sign of the Cross. Often the child knows nothing of the good God. The parents excuse themselves for this by saying that such instructions are the task of the catechists and other teachers of religion.

When religious instructions do not begin already with the

small child, in later years religion will not be grounded. What is the reason for today's religious indifference, this moral decadence? It is because children have not learned to deny themselves. This results in today's discontented persons who know nothing of restraint, who want to experience everything and enjoy every comfort. Therefore there is so much illicit sexuality, contraception and abortion. These unborn children cry to heaven for vengeance. In many places they outnumber the newly born children. Laws against abortion must become more strict, as even fourteen-year old girls are guilty. Every physician who, when examining, detects an abortion, is obliged to notify the competent authority; otherwise he burdens himself with an awful responsibility.

One who hasn't already learned as a child to deny himself will become selfish, uncharitable and domineering. That's why there is so much hatred and uncharitableness in the world. If we yearn for better times, we must first give a better upbringing to the children.

People sin frighteningly against charity, especially by slander and deceit. Where does it all start? In our thoughts. One must learn to ban all uncharitable thoughts immediately. One has to learn this as a child. Crush any uncharitable thought immediately and you will not judge uncharitably.

Every Catholic is obliged to help in the apostolate; one by his or her vocation; the other through good example. People complain that so many become corrupt through immoral talk and talk against faith. Why do they keep silent? Good people should also fight for their opinion and acknowledge being Christians. Has there ever been in the history of the Church a time when saving souls and Christian culture has been so urgently and imperatively the task of the laity, as today? The kingdom of God, Maria was told, should be again more sought for and propagated by all Christians; otherwise people will no longer be able to see the hand of Divine Providence in creation and its events. Care for the soul should not be pushed aside by excessive care for the body.

During the night of January 22, 1955, Maria Simma heard these words spoken very loud and distinct: "God demands atonement!" Much atonement can be made by voluntary sacrifices and prayer. If this is not done voluntarily, God will continue to obtain victims by force, but atonement must be made.

Conclusion

On the whole, there is question here of Maria Simma having a special vocation of grace in favor of the Poor Souls. This becomes clearly manifest in a note jotted down on November 21, 1954, which says: "Frequently the thought had come to me to send a Poor Soul to some other person, and I asked one of them why it did not go directly to its relatives; that would be much simpler than if I had to send messages. Thereupon came a Poor Soul and gave me a sharp reprimand, 'Do not sin against God's disposition. God distributes His graces to whom He wills. You will never be able to send a Poor Soul to another person. It is not due to any merits of yours that God permits us to come to you. As to merits, many others would deserve this much more than you. It is true that already as a child you gave much help to the Poor Souls, but that, too, was a great grace. Many another soul would have made better use of it than you. In addition to the souls who worked great miracles on earth there were still greater, hidden saints who did not have that power but who attained to greater holiness than the former. One should never forget: *God asks more from a soul who receives greater graces.* God wants us to ask for His graces. A good and persevering prayer pierces the clouds and will be heard in the manner that is best for the one praying.' "

I think that by this report I have given adequate description of the situation. I tried to report everything which I, in the time from All Saints' Day, 1953, until February 1955, learned from Maria Simma, and verified; and also that which I partly learned from her notes. There is here a question of an apostolate and help for the Poor Souls. Everyone may form his own judgment as it seems right to him. I ask only that whoever rejects these happenings will justly judge Maria Simma.

Sonntag, February 20, 1955
(signed)   Alfons Matt,
            Pastor in Sonntag

Maria Simma

My Personal Experiences with the Poor Souls

God is as
The One attained—Heaven
The One lost—Hell
The One who tests—Judge
The One who purifies—Purgatory

—Hans Urs von Balthasar

One should not reject from the outset the thought that God can permit a soul, in the moment when it is leaving the body, or a Poor Soul from purgatory, to make some kind of impression upon living persons. When God permits a soul from the other world to speak to one in this world, He does it always with holy designs concerning salvation. He wants by such extraordinary means to sanctify that soul—not to satisfy human curiosity or arouse fear and terror.

—Dr. I. Klug. *Der Katholische Glaubensinhalt*

If the souls in purgatory could by remorse and contrition become purified, they would pay their debt in a single moment; so enormous is the intensity of the contrition that would seize them as a consequence of the enlightenment they now have of the cause of the hindrance to their highest aim in life, their union with their love, their God.

—St. Catherine of Genoa, *Treatise on Purgatory*, Chapter 13.

Why Does God Permit It?

Some people wonder whether it is really possible that deceased persons can appear to the living and why God permits such extraordinary things. Certainly it is not to satisfy curiosity! If, through the Mercy of God, such an unwonted experience occurs, it always lies in the divine plan of salvation, and the various events have to be evaluated accordingly: For us still living on earth they are meant to be of spiritual usefulness and for the departed a great consolation because they will be more speedily released from their sufferings. All these facts are to motivate us to pray and sacrifice more for the Poor Souls and not to attach ourselves so much to earthly things.

There lies a great danger in the fact that people live too well. We must be more intent to provide for eternal life, for it is never-ending. Let us not attach our heart to temporal things; we cannot take any of those perishable things with us. The big estate, the prosperous business, the beautiful home—all that will pass away, perhaps sooner than we imagine; all that we can take with us are good works. It is true, here we have need of earthly goods for our living, but again—do not attach your heart upon them; that is what counts. That is the meaning and purpose of such appearances of Poor Souls as well as of any other private revelation. It is only for such a purpose that God permits these supernatural contacts; may the good and merciful God assist us with His grace and blessing. A soul to whom God wants to give some special grace often experiences this grace already in childhood, but often, also, only later. God's ways are unsearchable and marvelous. A great sinner may become a great saint, as we can see in the life of St. Augustine. A Saul becomes a St. Paul, and that very suddenly!

Caution in Regard to Private Revelations

It is often difficult for us to understand why the Catholic Church is so reserved when there is question of private revelations. That reservation is well founded, and it is good that it is so because the Church is the guardian of the truth. It is better that she does not declare cases as genuine rather than to declare a single one as genuine which in reality is not. On the other hand, she may not reject revelations which are in perfect accord with the teachings of Jesus Christ, even if the revelations are not yet thoroughly explored theologically.

I was called to Bishop Dr. Bruno Wechner, and he said, "I doubt whether the questioning of Poor Souls concerning deceased persons be God's will." I answered, "One day I asked a Poor Soul, 'How is it possible that you can give me information in answer to my inquiries?' The answer was, 'It is communicated to us through Mary, the Mother of Mercy.'"

The bishop was of the opinion that I really should not intervene in such cases; that there were things between heaven and earth which are not yet perfectly understood theologically, but which really exist. Finally, the bishop declared that—in the event of his being questioned—I could never expect him to declare my case as genuine. The Church could never do that as long as the respective person was still living; that's how strict the Church is, and we have to acknowledge this attitude as correct, for a soul on whom God had bestowed genuine, extraordinary favors, could become unfaithful to His grace; no one is ever safe from the deceits of the hellish enemy. For this reason such a soul needs, above all, a good spiritual director. This, he added, would be a protection against the snares of the devil.

To Publish or to Keep Secret

"Why do the Poor Souls come expressly to you?" I have frequently been asked. Certainly not because I am more pious. There are many people more pious than I am to whom no Poor Souls come. Supernatural happenings are not a measurement for holiness. The guiding principle for perfection is, and will ever be, charity—genuine, unselfish charity, love of God and neighbor. For love of others, suffer in imitating Jesus Christ. Without the cross and suffering we simply cannot live in this world. One of the Poor Souls once told me: "Our sufferings bring us the greatest blessings when we bear them with great patience and place them as an offering into the hands of our Blessed Mother, asking her to give it to whomever she wishes, because she knows best where it will serve best and is needed most."

Certainly it is much easier to exhort a person who is suffering to be patient than to bravely bear some painful or disagreable thing oneself. However, just because it is so difficult, suffering is of such great value.

I know of no special reason why the Poor Souls come just to me. I am sure that the Poor Souls go also to other persons; I, myself knew two here in Vorarlberg; they are now dead. I have no doubt that today there are many people to whom the Poor Souls go for help; however, they are known only to a few persons. They have been given a task different from mine.

It would be so much easier to keep everything secret rather than to bring it to the public and stand up for it. Few understand and, therefore, such persons are often disdained, even by priests. Many priests who are well educated think they understand everything, but God's ways are inscrutable. We need great humility; that is lacking so much nowadays.

I Wanted to Enter the Convent

Already as a child I felt that God was asking a special sacrifice from me. But what kind of sacrifice? When still in grammar school I wanted to find out. On my long way to get the milk, I had to pass by two hay stacks. I thought to myself that on this way the good God could really tell me what he wants from me so I have to arrange something with Him. I prayed, "Dear God, you can do anything, so when I pass by one or the other of these hay stacks, let there be lying a slip of paper which tells me what I should do." Again and again on my way I went by these stacks looking for such a slip, but always in vain. By and by I became impatient and said to the good God, "You know I am not at fault if I don't find the way you have destined for me."

After graduating from school I thought that it really seemed I should enter a convent; maybe that is what Our Lord wants. So at seventeen I entered Sacred Heart Convent in Hall/Tirol. After a year I had to leave because I lacked the necessary health.

Immediately I wanted to enter another convent. This time I tried the Dominican Sisters in Thalbach, near Bregenz, on the Bodensee. "We must tell you right away," Sister Superior said, "You are too frail for our convent." so I could not stay.

Later I became acquainted with the Franciscan Convent in Gaissau, from where Sisters are sent into the missions. "That's the convent where I belong," I thought to myself. "That is my special task—to lead other people to God. I am not talented enough to study to become a teacher, so I now shall enter a convent from where later on I can go to the missions." I said to Our Lord, "But now you have to help me to stay because I will not enter any other convent." In 1938 I entered there. I liked it very much. It is true, again and again the Sister Superior said to me, "You are really the frailest of us all." However, I was hoping that when the work in the fields would be over I would be able to overcome this.

Hardly had the harvest time ended when the superior said to me, "You are really too frail for us. I cannot keep you."

The First Apparitions

"Now all this trouble has been wasted," I thought. I couldn't find the way which God had destined for me, and God, Himself, didn't show it to me.

For quite a long time, spiritually I suffered from this; however I gathered strength from the thought: it isn't my fault; I tried everything possible.

From childhood on I had a great love for the Poor Souls. My mother, too, had great confidence in them and tried to impress upon us again and again, "If you have any great concern, go to the Poor Souls; they are most grateful and wonderful in helping us."

In 1940 the first Poor Soul came to me. I woke up because I heard someone walking up and down in my room. I looked up to see who was there. I wasn't easily frightened; rather I would have jumped into anyone's face than simply to give in to fear.

And then I saw a strange man in my room; he was slowly walking up and down. Brusquely and abruptly I asked him, "How did you get in here? What have you to do here?" He behaved as though he didn't hear me and continued walking up and down. "Who are you?" I asked, and again not receiving any answer, I jumped out of bed and tried to grab him. There was nothing! Just air.

I returned to bed and again heard him walking up and down. "Now I'm wide awake," I thought, "and see and hear this man. Why can't I grab him?"

Again I got up, slowly advanced toward him and tried to seize him, but again there was nothing but a void. Now I felt uneasy. I lay down again; it was about four o'clock in the morning. He did not return, but I couldn't sleep a wink.

After Mass I went to my spiritual director and told him everything.

"If anything like that happens again," he curtly instructed me, "don't ask 'Who are you?' but 'What do you want from me?'"

The following night the same man was back again. I asked, "What do you want of me?" The answer, "Have three Masses offered for me, then I shall be released!"

From this I knew that he was a Poor Soul. Reporting the incident to my confessor, he confirmed my opinion.

From 1940 until 1953, two or three souls came each year, mostly in November. I couldn't see in this any special apostolate. I kept my spiritual director informed. He was Father Alfons Matt, our pastor. He counseled me never to refuse a Poor Soul but to willingly accept everything.

Vicarious Sufferings

After a while the Poor Souls also asked me to suffer for them. There were great sufferings.

When a soul comes, it wakens me by knocking, calling, tugging, etc. I immediately ask, "What do you want?" or "What shall I do for you?" Only then can the soul tell me its needs. Thus one of them asked me, "Would you be willing to suffer for me?" That seemed strange to me because, so far, none had asked for that. I asked, "What have I to do?" The response was, "For three hours you will suffer great pains in your entire body but after these three hours you will be able to get up and do your work as though nothing had happened. By this you can shorten my purgatory by twenty years."

I accepted. Thereupon I was seized by such terrible pains that I hardly knew anymore where I was though I remained conscious of the fact that I had accepted these sufferings in atonement for some Poor Soul and that it should last for three hours. Then it struck me that these three hours must long since have ended; that it must rather be three days, if not three weeks. When everything was over and I inquired, I found that in reality it had been only three hours. Often I had to suffer for only five minutes, but, oh, what a long time that was!

Commissions By the Poor Souls Set the Thing in Motion

In 1954—it was the Marian Year—every night some Poor Souls appeared. At times they told me who they were, their names, where and when they had died. They gave me various messages for their relatives.

In this way the whole affair gradually became known, a thing that was very disagreeable to me. As far as I am concerned, no one besides my spiritual director would ever have come to know anything about it.

Frequently, I had to convey such messages to places entirely unknown to me. Occasionally, I also had to tell people to return ill-gotten goods, and exactly what. There were cases where not even all members of the family knew anything about it, and yet the message was correct.

The Poor Souls appeared also in the daytime, not only during the night.

After the close of the Marian Year the Poor Souls no longer came every night but on an average of two to three nights a week; sometimes they stayed away for an entire week. Most frequently they came on the First Saturday of the month or on a feast of Our Blessed Mother, also during Lent, but above all in Holy Week when many are permitted to come; likewise during November and in Advent.

Various Questions

Do I recognize the Poor Souls?

Those whom I have known during life I immediately recognize, but the others I don't unless they tell me who they are. Usually they appear in their working clothes.

Can one send a Poor Soul to some other person?

No, one cannot do that. Often I would have liked to do so, especially to send them to those people who make fun of such things and don't believe that Poor Souls can appear. I have also been asked whether one can summon the Poor Souls. No, I cannot do that; they simply come when God permits them to ask for their release.

Is it a sin if one does not believe in apparitions of the Poor Souls?

No. It is not a dogma and therefore one is not obliged to believe in it. However, one should not ridicule these things.

What Do the Poor Souls Know About Us?

The Poor Souls know much more about us and the events of our times than we think. They know, for instance, who is attending their funeral and whether one is praying for them or attends only to be seen without a word of prayer, as is often the case nowadays. And they know whether one leaves after having put the customary contribution in the basket without staying for Mass; the Mass would help the Poor Souls most of all. If one would devoutly attend Mass instead of accompanying the coffin to the cemetery, one would help these souls much more. So often people go only in order to be seen and that helps the Poor Souls very little.

The Poor Souls also know all we talk about them, what we do for them. They are much nearer to us than we think; they are very close to us.

What Will Help the Poor Souls?

Without doubt, the most precious help we can give is the Eucharistic Sacrifice; however, only insofar as the souls in question had appreciated it during life. In this respect, too, the word remains true, "What a man sows, he will reap." By the way, also weekday Masses are counted, and not only the obligatory Masses of Sundays and holy days.

37

Certainly not all can attend Mass on weekdays; people have to fulfill the duties of their state in life and duty comes first. But many could go without failing in their duties; for instance, one who is retired and lives close to the church, is healthy and can still easily arise and be around. But he says to himself, "On Sundays I am obliged to attend Mass, but not during the week, so I will not go."

Whoever thinks and acts like that will have to wait a long time after death until a Mass will be offered for him because he thought little of it during his lifetime.

If we cannot go ourselves, then let us send the school children as often as possible. In many places you no longer see the children in Mass on weekdays. If one would understand the value for eternity of a single Mass, the churches would be filled also on weekdays. In our dying hour, the Masses we have participated in with devotion will be our greatest treasure. They are of greater value to us than the Masses that will be offered for us after death.

Parents as well as educators complain that nowadays children have become very insolent and disobedient. That doesn't happen by accident; formerly children used to attend the daily school Mass; prayer and Communion gave them strength to be obedient and conscientious. No father, no mother, and no catechist can implant into the hearts of children what Jesus Himself gives them in Holy Mass and Communion.

I have at times been asked whether the burning of candles and vigil lights has any meaning and value. Certainly, especially when they have been blessed. And even if they have not been blessed, one has to consider that the candles and other lights have been bought for love of the departed ones, and every act of charity is of great value.

Holy Water, too, is an important means to help the Poor

Souls, if we use it with faith and confidence. However, it is all one whether we sprinkle a handful or only a single drop. It is best to frequently sprinkle a drop with a short prayer for the Poor Souls. It is very regrettable that in many homes one can no longer find a Holy Water font as thus the Poor Souls have to miss this great help.

Which Sins Receive the Severest Punishment?

Sins against charity, such as slander, calumnyy, irreconcilableness, quarrels because of greed and envy are severely punished in eternity. There is, for instance, a good-for-nothing; he could be a worthy person if he were treated with love and kindness. Beware of deriding and ridiculing such a person; it does great harm to our souls. Also, how often persons who are living alone complain that they receive so little help. There are, for instance, youngsters living in their neighborhood, hardly thirty feet away. It doesn't occur to them to shovel the deep snow to make a path for their old, helpless neighbor. And yet, in eternity, works of charity are given the highest reward.

How often people sin through uncharitable talk and judgment; one could write a whole book about that. If we would heed the admonition of Our Blessed Mother, "Be kind and good to everyone," we could convert most people and wouldn't have to fear communism. A single word can kill; a single word can heal. "Charity covers a multitude of sins." Above all, let us treat our enemies charitably. Christ tells us, "To be good to those who are good to us, even the pagans do as much." But to be good to those who are hostile to us, that is genuine Christian behavior; that is what Our Lord is expecting from us. Acting like that would convert many an enemy to a friend and we would save ourselves a long purgatory.

What Sufferings Do the Poor Souls Experience?

There is a thousandfold difference: There are as many kinds of purgatory as there are souls. Every soul is languishing for God, and, I think, that is the most piercing of all pains. Moreover, every soul will be punished in what and with what it had sinned. This is already partly the case while still on earth, where punishment often follows quickly on a person's heels: One who overeats gets a stomachache and becomes overweight; one who smokes too much incurs nicotine poisoning and cancer of the lungs, etc. Not a single soul would return from purgatory and continue to live the way it had lived before, returning to the darkness in which we are now immersed—because it now has a knowledge of which we have not the faintest idea.

The Poor Souls *want* purgatory, that purging process, as gold wants to cleanse itself from dross. Can we imagine a young girl who would like to participate at her first ball with soiled clothes and unkempt hair? A soul in purgatory has such an illuminating concept of God—God has appeared to it in such a radiant, dazzling beauty and purity—that all the powers of heaven would not suffice to cause this soul to present itself before God still bearing the smallest blemish. Only a soul resplendent and perfect in beauty would dare to appear before Eternal Light and Divine Perfection, beholding God face to face.

Why I Give Talks

"You are to go everywhere you are asked," the Poor Souls tell me. "That is your apostolate." Vatican Council II also asks that lay people be more active in various apostolates. In Confirmation, every Catholic is given the duty to stand up for faith and truth, in proportion to the gift of grace received. Therefore, it is my duty, also, to give these talks. Even some priests do not understand this and, therefore, do not give permission for these talks which people want. Let us pray for them. I do not accept payment for talks or discussions, only remuneration for travel and board. One reproachingly said to me that for sure I also receive voluntary donations which are worth more than the traveling expenses. Yes, I do, but I do not use it for myself; it is put into the "Poor Souls Box," the little poor box into which every dime above the just sum goes. This belongs to the Poor Souls who beg for a Mass or for a contribution toward some good work.

I am accustomed to a frugal life. During the years of my childhood, when I attended school, we had for dinner and supper nothing but a dish of soup and a piece of bread. Nevertheless, all eight of us children grew up in good health. Often people would be healthier if they would live simpler lives.

People ask me also what kind of schools I attended that I can give such talks. I had only eight years of grammar school, but through my relations with the Poor Souls I have learned much. They also brought about a change in me. Moreover, I have great confidence in the Holy Spirit. Not before we really confidently invoke the Holy Spirit shall we experience how powerful is His help. Also, how very important is His assistance in the field of education! Therefore, I cannot advise parents and educators enough to ask the Holy Spirit for enlightenment.

Should We Forgive Others Even After Their Death?

Once a farmer came to me and complained, "I am building a stable. Each time, when the wall has reached a certain height, it collapses on the other side. We examined everything and cannot find a flaw. I cannot help but think that there is something unnatural involved. What shall we do?"

I asked him, "Is there perhaps some deceased person who had something against you? Who was hostile to you?" He answered, "Well, yes, there was someone. Right away the thought has occurred to me that it can be only he. He doesn't leave me in peace even after having gone to the grave!"

"That man only wants you to forgive him," I declared, "and nothing else."

"What! I should forgive that man who in this life did me so much harm—and help him now so he can just fly into heaven! No! No! Let him make up for his offense." I had to appease the farmer, "But he won't fly immediately into heaven through that! He will have to atone until the end, but he will bear it easier, and he will give you no rest until you have forgiven him from the heart."

He didn't want to accept this, so I asked him, "What do you pray in the Our Father? 'Forgive us our trespasses as we forgive those who trespass against us.' There, then, you practically say to God, 'You may not forgive me because I do not forgive my neighbor!' "

"Well, yes, I can see that now," he had to admit. Finally, I succeeded in having him declare, "All right, in God's name I forgive him, that God will also forgive me."

In Which Way Do I Receive the Answers?

Only on the First Saturday of a month or a feast of Our Blessed Mother may I inquire whether a soul is still in purgatory or not. When a soul appears and, after having declared what it still needs for its release, it does not leave, I know that I may ask a question. However, I do not receive the answer from that same soul simply because in the meantime it will have been released if someone has complied with its request.

Rather, the answer will be given by some other soul who may come to ask for help in obtaining its release. After having mentioned its request, it will then say, "The soul of X is still in purgatory," or, "has been released."

Thereupon I look up that name in my notebook to find out who gave me that name so that I can send on the information.

At times it may take two or three years until I receive an answer, but often less than that, depending upon what God permits. I don't think that the Poor Souls may disclose whether someone has been condemned to hell, but beware of drawing from that the conclusion that there is no hell.

Oh, there is a hell and already many souls are in it! When someone asks me the surest means not to be condemned to hell, I answer, "Be very humble. A humble soul will not go to hell, but a proud person is in danger of being eternally lost."

Is the Plenary Indulgence For the Hour of Death of Any Avail?

Once a man came with an inquiry about his deceased wife. The answer was, "She is still in purgatory." This seemed strange since this woman had belonged to several pious associations in which one could gain a plenary indulgence at the hour of death. One would, therefore, have supposed that she was no longer in purgatory. I asked a Poor Soul to explain this.

The answer was, "To gain a plenary indulgence for oneself, the soul must be entirely free of every attachment to what is earthly; only then can she gain the indulgence, but much is required for this. For instance, a mother of five children lies dying and now she should pray, 'O my God, I will only what you will, life or death, entirely as you will!' To do this requires much, and one will not succeed unless one has lived accordingly."

If Someone is Up to Mischief?

Someone requested information from me concerning a certain person whose name, and year of birth and death he sent. The answer was, "Is still in purgatory." Thereupon I received the sarcastic answer, "There you have it! Now one can see that this is a fraud; that woman is still living!"

I wondered how it was possible that a Poor Soul would tell me that person was in purgatory. I went to my spiritual director and told him, "I no longer shall accept inquiries; something is wrong there!"

With calmness and composure he answered, "When you again talk with a Poor Soul, demand an explanation and say, 'In the name of Jesus I command you to tell me why you gave me a wrong answer. That person is still alive.'" I did as I was told and received the following information:

"That answer was not given by a Poor Soul."

"But then, by whom?"

The Poor Soul replied, "It was the hellish enemy in the form of a Poor Soul!"

"Has that happened before?"

"When an inquiry was made in the proper way, you received from us the correct answer, but when someone is up to mischief, then the devil is empowered to have a finger in the pie, but only then."

Our pastor to whom I reported this said, "Yes, I thought that here the evil one was involved. This is no joking matter; one must strictly adhere to the truth. The devil is the father of lies. When one deviates from the truth, the devil has his sphere of influence.

A Village Becomes Excited

In the year 1954 a man came to me and inquired about two deceased persons. "I am anxiously awaiting the answer," he said.

"Why?" But he wouldn't say any more, only that he would return for the answer. As it was the Marian Year, I received the answer rather soon. After only a month I was able to inform him, "Mrs. S. has been released and Mr. H. is still in purgatory."

He shook his head, "That can't be true. Mrs. S. died in the hospital as a result of an abortion; and she should be still in purgatory! Mr. H., however, used to be the first and the last in church; and he should be released."

"It is now the Marian Year," I responded, "and I receive so many answers at one time that I may have confused some of them. I shall inquire again." And so I did. The answer, "You noted it correctly; that was the truth."

When I forwarded the answer to the inquirer, he no longer wanted to believe the whole matter.

This man came from the same village as Mrs. S. and Mr. H. and half the village was excited about the answer concerning these two persons, but I could not change anything in the answer.

Then it happened that from the same village there came a woman to me who also had been well acquainted with Mrs. S. She was of a very different opinion than those excited people. "Because your answer was as it is," she told me, "I am confirmed in my belief in the correctness of your answers." She told me this was the special purpose why she came to me. Then she continued:

"I knew Mrs. S., one could say, as though she had been my own sister. It is true; she was morally weak, but she suffered deeply from that for it was with her mostly due to heredity. Yes, she died of an abortion, but the priest who assisted her at death had to remark, 'I hope I shall die in such a state of deep contrition as this woman.' She died before Mr. H. and was given a church funeral. Mr. H., it is true, was the first and the last in church, but he was constantly criticizing people. But what mostly aroused my indignation was the fact that, concerning Mrs. S., no one showed himself as shocked as Mr. H., who even made the remark that such a wretch did not belong in their cemetery."

I thanked the woman for her information and I said to her, "Now everything is clear to me. Our Lord does not want us to judge others. Mr. H. condemned that poor woman; he can be glad that God was so merciful to him that he has been saved at all, for it is a very dangerous thing to condemn someone." We may not do that. There may be twenty persons doing the same thing, judging from the exterior, and yet guilt may be different for each one, depending on the motives and background, for example, education, heredity, knowledge, health, treatment by others, environment. These we simply cannot judge.

Do Children Also Go to Purgatory?

Yes, even children, even preschool children may go to purgatory. As soon as a child knows that something isn't right to do and yet does it, it contracts guilt. Of course such children haven't a long or severe purgatory because full knowledge is lacking. However, by no means say that a child doesn't understand yet; a child understands more than we think; they have a much more delicate conscience than an adult.

What is the fate of unbaptized children? These children, too, have a heaven. They are happy but do not enjoy the beatific vision. However, they know so little about this that they think they have the most wonderful state that there is.

What about those who commit suicide? Are they lost? No, in most cases not, because they were then not sound in mind and, therefore, not responsible. Much more responsible are those through whose fault they resorted to suicide.

Do non-Catholics go to purgatory? Yes, also those who did not believe in purgatory. However, they do not suffer in purgatory as much as does a Catholic, for they did not have as many means of grace. Of course, neither will they enjoy the same eternal happiness.

Can the Poor Souls help themselves? No, they cannot help themselves in the least, but they can help us very much if we ask them for help.

A Traffic Accident in Vienna

A Poor Soul told me, "I had a fatal traffic accident with my motorcycle in Vienna because I did not observe the traffic laws; that was my doom."

I asked him, "Were you prepared for eternity?"

"I really hadn't been prepared," he admitted, "but God gives everyone who does not presumptuously and with insolence sin against Him, two to three minutes in which he can make an Act of Contrition; only one who says, 'I won't!' is lost."

He also made some interesting and instructive comments: "In such a case, people often say, 'Well, I think this was the hour destined for him to die!' That is not right; it is true only in cases where someone is killed entirely without his fault. In such a case one may rightly say, 'It was his destiny.' According to God's disposition, I could have lived an additional thirty more years—only then my hour would have come. Therefore, we may never without necessity endanger our lives."

A Hundred Year Old Woman of the Street

One day in 1954, about three o'clock in the afternoon, I was on my way to Marul. In the forest, just before one reaches our neighboring town, I met an old woman. She looked so old that I thought she must be at least a hundred years old. When I greeted her in a friendly way, she said, "Why do you greet me? No one greets me anymore!"

I tried to console her, "You deserve a greeting just as well as anyone else!"

Then she started to complain, "No one still acknowledges

me; no one gives me anything to eat, and I have to sleep in the street."

"That can't be," I thought, "she must not be quite right in her mind." I tried to explain to her that such a thing couldn't happen.

"But certainly!" she exclaimed. I thought that because she was so old she might be a burden and, therefore, people might not like to keep her for any length of time. Thereupon I invited her to lodge with me.

"O, thank you! But I can't pay you."

"That's no obstacle, but you must take things as they are. I have only plain accommodations but, after, all, it's better than sleeping in the street."

Thereupon she thanked me, "May God reward you! Now I am released!" and she disappeared.

Until then I had not noticed that she was a Poor Soul. Apparently some time in her life, when she had been obliged to help, she had refused to help and now she had to wait until someone voluntarily offered to help her.

An Encounter in a Train

"Do you know me?" I was asked by a Poor Soul. I had to say that I didn't.

"But we have met. In 1932 you went by train to Hall and were my companion in the compartment."

Now everything was clear to me. He was the one who at that time in the train sharply attacked the Church and religion. Although I was only 17 at the time, I took courage and told him that he could not be a good person if he spoke so degradingly.

"You're nothing more than a youngster," he said in defense, "and I should take advice from you!"

"Nevertheless, I'm cleverer than you are," I boldly answered. Thereupon he lowered his head and didn't say another word. When he got off the train, I begged Jesus, "Do not let this soul be lost." "That prayer has saved me," the Poor Soul declared, "otherwise I would have been lost."

A Woman Saves a Village

In 1954 we had a frightful avalanche in our area. Shortly afterward, in our neighborhood of Fontanella a Mrs. Stark died; she had been ill for 30 years. People were talking that time about a similar catastrophe that had happened a hundred years before, but which had been even worse. After that destruction, they said, a forest was begun in Fontanella to protect the village. During the avalanche of 1954, this protecting forest was completely swept away. A few trees stopped the powerful snowslide, otherwise half the village would have been swept away.

As mentioned, shortly after the catastrophe, Mrs. Stark died. I was then told by the Poor Souls, "No one but this woman has saved the village, and that through her prayers and sacrifices." She had offered up all her sufferings for the good of the community and thereby had obtained many graces for it. This she could not have achieved during days of good health. Through patient suffering one can obtain more graces than by prayer.

I know what it means to suffer. It is just because it is so difficult that it is of such great value.

Do not always look upon suffering as a punishment! We can

make it a sacrifice of atonement, and not only for ourselves but above all for others.

Christ was the most innocent and He suffered most in atonement for our sins. In like manner all our sufferings are to contribute toward the salvation of souls. Only in heaven shall we know the great blessings we have obtained by patiently suffering in union with Christ.

The most effective way to offer up our sufferings is to place them in the hands of Our Blessed Mother so that she can apply them to whom she wishes. She knows best who needs them most.

Scrubbing Pail; Black Hand; Descecrating a Crucifix

"What are you going to do with that scrubbing pail?" I asked a woman I met on the street who was holding a scrubbing pail in her hand.

"That's my key to heaven," she responded with a radiant face. "I didn't pray much during life and seldom went to church, but once, before Christmas, I cleaned a poor old woman's house without charge—that saved me!" Another indication that what matters again and again is charity.

I shall never forget my encounter with a priest whose right hand was all black. I inquired the reason for it. He answered, "I should oftener have made use of the priestly blessing. Tell that to every priest with whom you come in contact. They should bless more frequently. By that they can diffuse great blessings and ward off much evil power.

* * *

Once a soul came to me and told me what it would need for its release. Then it added, "If one will do this for me, I shall be content." It didn't say anything else, only when and where it had died.

I forwarded the message to the family, whom I did not know. At first those people were skeptical and wanted to know whether every Poor Soul said, "If one will do this for me, I shall be content."

Until now," I answered, "this is the first soul using that expression."

Thereupon they wanted to know why it might have said that. I told them that I did not know.

"But we know," they remarked thoughtfully. "It was the habitual expression of our father. He always said, 'If you do that (or will do it that way), I shall be content.' That is the reason we believe you."

They were people who no longer attended Sunday Mass, being of the opinion that since it was a precept of the Church, they were not obliged by God. I then explained to them that in eternity a command of the Church is assessed just as severely as a commandment of God, the only difference being that the Church can abolish or change one of her commands, a thing that is impossible for her in regard to a commandment of God.

* * *

"I was a blasphemer," a man confessed to me. "In my rage I trampled on a crucifix, thinking, 'If there were a God, He would not permit this.' But God is not mocked. Immediately I became paralyzed. That is what saved me."

He told me what his wife should do for him and how one could alleviate his purgatory.

His wife no longer went to church, but the message I brought to her made a deep impression upon her.

"Only my husband and I knew that he had sacrilegiously treated a crucifix; I didn't talk about it to anybody, and my husband was unable to communicate it to anybody. If an unknown person can give me this information, I cannot help but believe it." And she returned to the Church.

* * *

One day a doctor came and complained that he had to suffer because he had shortened the lives of patients by injections so that they no longer would have to suffer so much. He said that sufferings are of infinite value to the soul when patiently borne. It is permissible to alleviate great pains, but it is wrong to shorten life by chemical means.

Stolen Goods

One day a visitor came; while he was still in the hall, I heard him loudly scolding. I opened the door of my room to see what was going on. Then I saw a man in the hall who asked in a disdainful tone of voice, "Where is this creator of Poor Soul fantasies?"

"Just walk in," I answered, "but there is no creator of Poor Soul fantasies here." Thereupon he came straight to the point, "Did Mr. E. appear to you?" The visitor was one of Mr. E.'s relatives and I had had to inform him to return some stolen goods. When I answered in the affirmative, he started to rave and rant, saying that there was no truth to it, that it was only extortion, swindle, etc.

What stolen goods should we give back?" he wanted to know exactly now.

I told him, "I do not know. I was only instructed to tell the family to return the stolen goods. You yourself must know which goods." He then told me exactly what they were. From his manner of speaking I could soon see that his Christian faith didn't amount to much. He cursed and swore and used abusive language about the pope, the Church, and religion. Calmly I explained matters to him. Thereupon he became more acquiescent and said, "If that is how matters stand, I have to start leading a better life. I no longer trusted any priest, but now I cannot but believe in God again for you could not possibly have known that there were stolen goods on our property; not even all the members of our family knew about it."

Another time a woman came to me saying, "I had to suffer 30 years in purgatory because I did not allow my daughter to enter a convent." If God gives parents a child and He then gives that child a vocation to the priesthood or the religious life, those parents who oppose the vocation will have a grave responsibility.

I learned from the Poor Souls that many young men have a vocation to the priesthood but their parents resist; these parents will have to give an account for this.

The Woman with the Severest Purgatory

I received a letter from a man who told me that his wife had died a year ago. Since then, every night he heard a knocking in his room. Wouldn't I please come to try to find out the cause?

I drove over but told the man that I wasn't sure whether I

would receive any information; perhaps his wife was not allowed as yet to give any sign; we would have to leave that to Divine Providence.

I then stayed overnight in that room. About 11:30 P.M. a rattling and rumbling started. I immediately asked, "What do you want me to do for you?"

I didn't see anyone nor did I receive an answer. I thought that this woman had not yet permission to make herself known. Then, about five minutes later, I heard a frightening stamping and trampling. A huge animal came toward me, something that as yet had not happened before. It was a hippopotamus. Right away I sprinkled some holy water and asked, "How can I help you?" Again, no answer; it was simply uncanny. Then the evil one mingled in. He came in the form of a horrible, ghastly, giant-snake which wound itself round the animal in such a way as to strangle it—then all of a sudden everything vanished.

I greatly feared that this woman might be lost. Shortly after, another Poor Soul appeared in human form as they usually do. She consoled me, saying, "Do not fear. That woman is not lost, but she is in the most torturous purgatory there is." And the soul explained that this woman had lived for decades in enmity with another woman, and she had been the cause of it. The other woman had often tried to make peace with her, but she had refused. Even in her dying hour she harshly repulsed her and that was how she had died.

Here again we have proof how severely God punishes hostile behavior which is diametrically opposed to charity. Frequently, during this life quarrels happen, but let us take great care quickly to make peace again. Let us forgive as soon as possible. Nothing is better than charity. Charity covers a multitude of sins. We cannot stress that too much.

Killed by an Avalanche

At the time of the great avalanche in 1954, a young man, 20 years old, who lived in a house that had been protected from the avalanche, heard cries for help during the night. Immediately, he rose and was about to run out to help. His mother tried to stop him, saying that for a change some other people should help, and that, just then when the avalanches were roaring, it was too dangerous.

The young man, however, would not be stopped; he rushed to where the cries came, but on the way he, himself, was buried under an avalanche and died.

Already the second night after the accident he came to me and asked to have three Masses offered for him. His family was surprised that he would be released that quickly because he hadn't been especially fervent about his religion.

To me, however, this young man confided that God had been so merciful to him because he had died in an act of charity; had he lived, he would not again have had such a happy hour of death.

Let us never be depressed when such accidents happen. We never know the good purpose it serves. People say, "How could that happen to such a good boy or to such a good girl?" I have known many a good boy or a good girl who later on went astray. God alone knows what those good young people would have become. Only in eternity shall we fully understand God's good providence for us.

Satan in Disguise

Once a Poor Soul came and demanded of me, "Do not accept the next soul!"

My spiritual director had told me to accept every soul; therefore I asked, "Why should I not accept the next soul?"

"It will need such great sufferings," was the answer, "that you will not be able to bear them."

"Then the good God should not let it come to me."

The reply was flung at me, "God will prove whether you will obey or not!"

Whenever I am confused or uncertain, I call upon the Holy Spirit; he never fails me. Immediately, the thought came to me that it could be the devil and I quickly determined to challenge him. "If you are the evil one, I command you, in the name of Jesus, to leave me!" Suddenly, there was a scream and the apparition disappeared. Now I knew that it had been the devil who had appeared in the form of a Poor Soul.

In our church, on days when there is a Funeral Mass at nine o'clock, Holy Communion is distributed at seven o'clock. On one such day I was in church at 6:45 A.M. Usually there were two or three other persons, but on this day I was alone. Suddenly our pastor came into the church in great agitation. In his excitement he did not genuflect; he approached me and said, "Today you may not receive Holy Communion," and quickly left again, without genuflecting.

I couldn't understand this and prayed the rosary. Then, shortly before seven o'clock, my spiritual director calmly entered the church. I expected him to leave right away since I was not permitted to receive Holy Communion and there was no other person there. Contrary to my expectation he went into the sacristy. I looked around to see whether someone else had come in but no one else was there. I went into the sacristy and asked, "Why may I not receive Holy Communion today?"

"Who said that?"

"You yourself told me that I may not receive Holy Communion today."

He wanted to know when he was supposed to have told me that.

Thereupon I described the whole incident to him. He reassured me, "Don't be disconcerted. I have not been in the church until now. That was the evil one. Come now to receive Holy Communion."

I knew a Mrs. Maria Graf in Appenzell, a simple farmer's wife to whom once in a while Our Blessed Mother appeared, giving her messages. One day Mrs. Graf came to me to ask my advice. On the one hand she felt obliged to make the messages known to the world; on the other hand the bishop requested that she say nothing.

I asked her, "Can you frequently talk to Our Blessed Mother?" When she answered in the affirmative, I advised her to ask Our Blessed Mother what she should do for Our Blessed Mother knew that the bishop had forbidden publicity about it. Mrs. Graf did as she was advised and received the answer, "Obey your bishop! I myself shall take care to make it known."

Mrs. Graf obeyed. Almost no one in Appenzell believed in her charism; even her husband was doubtful, but no one can obstruct God's plans. Shortly after Mrs. Graf's death, on February 19, 1954, a sick person was miraculously cured through Mrs. Graf's intercession. Then people became aroused. They came to her husband and begged him to make a search to find out whether his wife had left any writings. They found her notes, in which Our Blessed Mother several times expressed the wish that every day people should pray the rosary for the conversion of sinners—that this would be very powerful in frustrating the attacks of the devil.

Shortly after I heard this, I received two letters with almost identical contents—that there was something out of the ordinary happening in their homes; to all appearances the devil had a hand in it.

I decided to immediately sit down to write these two persons, advising them to daily pray the rosary for the conversion of sinners. That was on December 16, 1964, in bright daylight. I took two sheets of paper and placed them in the center of the table with the envelopes beside them. I am accustomed to write the address on the envelope first and then the letter. While I was writing the address on the first envelope, I heard—a loud hissing. I was terrified; the hellish fiend was standing beside me. He snatched the two sheets, pulling them to the edge of the table, leaving a burn-mark on each of them—evidence of the power of the rosary as a weapon against the devil.

Exhortations of the Poor Souls

Maria Simma often received exhortation and practical advice from the Poor Souls. Here is a brief list:

The Most Blessed Sacrament no longer receives proper reverence. In many modern churches it is no longer the focus-point. Images and statues are often a mockery of what they represent.

It is also a lack of humility and reverence to request that people receive Holy Communion standing, without making a genuflection. This does not mean that it may not be done by the sick and elderly. However, whoever wishes to receive Holy Communion kneeling must be given the opportunity to do so, as Pope Paul VI expressly requested.

Praying the rosary should be cultivated.

The rosary is very powerful; Mary is the Help of Christians.

* * *

Everywhere I give offense when, commissioned by the Poor Souls, I say that through indecent dress immorality is promoted. It is a serious matter and women have a great responsibility in this regard.

The Poor Souls also say that already at conception the human soul is present.

The Poor Souls also recommend that a last testament be made in good time. How often relatives and descendants quarrel because no testament was made or was not made with justice.

It is very important that everyone contribute toward building up the Kingdom of God. Parents have to give an account if they do not teach their children to actively contribute. Young people become guilty if they shirk good deeds because of love of ease and comfort.

Erection of a Chapel

A Poor Soul remarked that Our Blessed Mother desired to have a little chapel erected in Sonntag, and minutely described the location, a place where in former times there had been a wayside shrine of Our Blessed Mother. This little shrine had been removed when a road was constructed there. The promise had been made to replace it, but, as usually happens, the promise was forgotten. Now, on that spot was to be erected a chapel large enough so that the Eucharistic Sacrifice could be celebrated there.

I informed my spiritual director who immediately accepted the request because he indeed remembered that on that particular location a wayside shrine had stood in former times. I myself was ignorant of this; only older people still remembered.

The chapel was to be built with donations. Difficulties arose in the community. People could not understand why the chapel was to be built in a location where there were only two houses and not in an area where there were several houses. At the request of my spiritual director, I inquired about this, asking a Poor Soul whether the chapel might be built in the little hamlet of Türtsch which had more townspeople.

The answer was, "If the people of Türtsch want to have a chapel, they must pay for it themselves; they may not use any money that has already been contributed.

Especially on the initiative of my spiritual director, Pastor Matt, the chapel was erected on the location designated by Our Blessed Mother. In Vorarlberg there was not as yet a little chapel in honor of "The Virgin of the Poor of Banneaux"; therefore, Our Blessed Mother desired this statue for the chapel. Later on, the priest from Banneaux himself brought the statue which had been blessed in Banneaux, Belgium, to Sonntag.

When the chapel was finished, through a Poor Soul our Blessed Mother requested that a picture be hung in the chapel which would depict her as "Mother of Mercy for the Poor Souls," but it should be a picture of natural beauty, not a contorted work of modern art. I asked Our Blessed Mother's help to find a good painter. Shortly after, a Polish priest, Father Stanislaus Skudrzyk, S.J., came to me. When I told him about my search, he said that he knew a good artist in Cracow, Professor Adolf Hyla, who would be able to paint a truly beautiful picture.

This Polish Jesuit priest, who for years had been living in Hamburg, now took everything into his hands, including the financing of the painting.

The transportation of the picture from Cracow, via London, to Sonntag took place without incident. In Mary's month, May 1959, the chapel was dedicated, and since then is open to all people as a place of pilgrimage and a memorial for the Poor Souls. The location of this little shrine, high above the last village in the Grossen Walsertal, the solitude and peaceful stillness and the marvelous panorama of the pre-Alpine valley with its green mountain pastures and their fragrance of wild flowers and the chirping of crickets, is a sheer delight.

If you desire to retire to a little corner in God's untouched nature for silent converse with Him, you will find it here.

New Experiences

When a book has an edition of 100,000 copies within six years, and is published in five languages, this is, for the author as well as for the publishing company, an event which fills them with satisfaction and with gratitude to God. It also induced us to invite Maria Simma to come to our publishing house. On this occasion, new events came up for discussion; some are given below.

The great demand for the book shows that the faithful have a genuine need to be informed about what concerns eschatology. Perhaps Divine Providence conferred this charism on a soul of our time for this special reason because even many priests "can no longer stand the sound teaching" and hardly ever preach on death, judgment, purgatory and resurrection. The more Christianity is failing in this regard, the more occult practices, such as spiritism, soothsaying, yes, and even satanism, are gaining in popularity.

At the end of this section, an event is related under the title, "Who Was the Victor?" which is typical for the phenomenon of Maria Simma. This event (names of persons and the town are known to the publisher) is another manifestation of how God, time and again, uses weak instruments to confound the strong. One cannot deny the fact that simple, modest Maria Simma is successful in certain matters, namely conversions, in which nowadays even many clerics fail. By this fact she proves that she possesses the most important criterion which Christ has for the Kingdom of God, namely, "By their fruits you will know them."

Does the End Justify the Means?

One day a woman, who is still living, came to me to confide her troubles to me, "My husband, to whom our little boy was deeply attached, died early. Now the boy has gone completely astray. If you would tell the boy that his father had come to you saying that he had to undergo great sufferings because the boy had gone astray, my son without hesitation would change his life because he could not tolerate the thought that because of him his father was suffering."

I said to her, "Well, pray to the good God that He may permit the father to come to me and say that."

"All right, but even if the father does not come, you could say that anyway."

"No, that would mean telling an outright lie," I responded.

"True, but the boy would become converted."

We know, however, that this may not be done. In such matters one must strictly abide by the truth. If one does that, one will always come through all right.

The father did not come, so I couldn't tell the boy that he did; perhaps the son wouldn't have changed his life anyhow.

Become a Priest in Our Time or Not?

Once before I pointed out the great responsibility parents have when God calls one of their children into His special service. The father of a family once said to me, "At the present time I would not let my son become a priest."

"Why not?"

"Oh! You yourself know the situation today; there are modern priests who teach things that are no longer Catholic. I would not entrust my boy to them. I would, therefore, prefer that he does not become a priest."

I asked him to ponder well the following: Until your son can become a priest, twelve or thirteen years will have to pass. By then we shall have a different time, of that I am very sure. This time of dissolution will not remain. Every Council is accompanied by at least some confusion, and never yet has there been such a great Council of the Church as Vatican II. Yet the great confusion is not the fault of the Council. Most guilty are the cardinals, bishops and priests who no longer obey the Holy Father.

I Was Perspiring from Fear

A woman invited me to come to her for a discussion. She asked me, "Will a Poor Soul come to you tonight?"

"I don't know," was my answer. "I never know in advance whether a soul is coming or not."

She then said, "As there are other patients at this spa who would like to hear your experiences, would you sleep in our dormitory?"

As among them there were two persons with heart diseases, I firmly refused. As she continued urging me, we finally agreed that I would sleep in the adjoining room, leaving the door ajar. I thought, "As our Lord will not allow anything to happen, all of them together would not hear anything."

The next morning I noticed that our hostess looked very serious and changed. When I inquired whether she did not feel well, she said, "I am not ill, but I must ask you, 'Did a Poor Soul come here last night?' "

"Yes, but why?"

She then asked, "Did this Poor Soul pray an 'Our Father'?"

"She couldn't hear that," I thought, so I pretended as though nothing had happened.

Then she admitted with a trembling voice, "I heard someone pray the 'Our Father' and it sounded as though it came from a deep cavern."

I was greatly surprised. "Then you are the first person who has heard a Poor Soul talking with me," I told her.

It is interesting that she heard the voice as if coming from a deep cavern since the way the Poor Soul had prayed with me had seemed quite normal. Moreover, I had prayed silently in order not to disturb those sleeping in the other room, thinking that they wouldn't hear the Poor Soul anyhow.

"I was perspiring from fear," the woman added, "and was glad that you did not sleep in our room."

A Teaching Sister with a Sense of Humor

I knew a teaching Sister in the Tirol, a good Sister who became ill and suffered with great patience. After a year I learned that she was in a sanatorium and I decided to pay her a visit. When I was with her, she said, "Say, why does the good God not hear my prayer? I am urgently needed in our school!"

"Well, do you know, Sister," I answered, trying to console her, "you must not forget that sufferings are the greatest proof of God's love for us."

"Oh!" she jokingly remarked, "it wouldn't be so bad then if for a little while He would show me a little less of His love!"

Confession of Sins Cannot Be Ignored

In many places, Confession, the Sacrament of Reconciliation, has also been discarded. It is a sacrament which Christ, and not the Church (as many maintain), has instituted. For Christ has said,

> Receive the Holy Spirit!
> For those whose sins you forgive,
> they are forgiven;
> For those whose sins you retain,
> they are retained.
>   (John 20:23)

Therefore the sins must be told; how otherwise could the priest decide whether he can and may forgive them, or not?

Someone said to me, "But Christ did not say that one has to go into the confessional."

"That's true; Christ did not say that. If you prefer, you may tell your sins to the priest and express your contrition before all the people. The priest can then absolve you outside the confessional; but the sins have to be told."

Here and there attempts are being made to supplant individual confession by penitential services; in such parishes the number of confessions is rapidly declining. There has been a wrong development. Rome as well as our Austrian bishops have clearly declared that in a penitential service no absolution of grave sins is possible. A penitential service is, therefore, never a substitute for individual confession.

In many places no longer are the First Communicants required to go to confession. This should not be. Already twice the Holy Father has declared that First Confession has to precede First Communion. Unfortunately, many priests no longer obey the Holy Father; that will take its toll.

Again and again, the Poor Souls request prayers for our Holy Father. Nowadays one must strictly adhere to the Holy Father and follow one's own conscience.

In Ulm I met some fifteen year old children who had not yet gone to confession. When I questioned them about this they said, "Before our First Communion we were not allowed to go to confession; in the sixth grade we were permitted to go. We said to one another, 'Now do you have any other sins that you did not have earlier?' 'Not really, excepting for some quarelling and disobeying.' 'Well, then!' we said to each other, 'Either we should have gone to confession before our First Communion, or else not at all. Now we won't go anymore!'"

Yet First Confession before First Communion is so important also for forming a right conscience. Many innovators did not obey their bishops and disarranged everything in a self-willed way. Now they must experience how the faithful, and especially the children, no longer obey them.

Who Was the Victor?

A manufacturer in southern Germany invited me to give a lecture. When I arrived, he said, "A year ago you gave a talk in a neighboring town. By chance I saw the poster announcing your lecture and I thought, 'Well! Is that possible; is there still such nonsense!' Suddenly the thought came to me, 'Truly speaking, I have nothing special to do at present and could go to find out what this nonsense is about.' So I went and took a seat in the rear. Unexpectedly, it was an hour of grace for me; it occurred at the passage where you said, 'As long as a man is alive, it is never too late; he can still make up for everything. Yes, he can even surpass everything. By great zeal he can make up for what he had neglected in the past.' For years I had not entered a church; now the love of God got hold of me and changed my life. My firm determination was, 'This woman must give a talk in our town too; I shall take care of that.'"

It was useless for him to see his pastor about this matter because he knew the pastor was not in favor of such affairs. He, therefore, contacted the town council who rented the town hall to him for three hundred marks. Scarcely had the announcement of the talk appeared in newspapers and on posters, than the pastor called up the manufacturer, saying, "What are you doing without my permission?" He answered, "For the time being we still have freedom of speech and conscience, as for the rest, Father, do not worry, I shall not harm a soul."

"Attack is the best defense," the pastor thought and declared, "I shall immediately publish a notice in the newspaper that no one should attend this lecture."

"Yes, Father," the manufacturer calmly replied, "You may do that, and I shall invoke all the Guardian Angels of this town for their help; then we shall see who will be the victor."

The pastor wrote the notice, but it arrived an hour too late to be printed and appeared in the paper only the day following my talk.

The hall had been crowded to overflowing. Fortunately there had been an efficient loudspeaking system so that contact could even be made with several buses which were crowded with people who had not been able to get into the hall.

The following day, when people read the pastor's notice in the newspaper, many laughed heartily and some called up the pastor, suggesting that he himself attend such a talk first, before exposing himself to ridicule.

Appendix

Purgatory and Prayers for the Dead*

Basis of Devotion Traced Through Scripture, Tradition and Reason

"Why do Catholics pray for the dead?" is a question frequently asked by our non-Catholic fellow citizens. Since the practice of praying for the souls of the deceased is based upon the doctrine of purgatory which was abandoned by the Reformers in the sixteenth century, and is now practically unknown among their followers, the latter are naturally at a loss to understand the Catholic custom of praying for their departed brethren, or as it is commonly called "the devotion to the poor souls." The Church keeps this devotion before the eyes of her children by setting aside the second of November as All Souls' Day, permitting her priests to celebrate three Masses on that day for the souls of the departed, and by designating the entire month of November as the month of special devotion for the poor souls. Let us invite our non-Catholic friends to investigate with us the basis of this devotion in Scripture, tradition and in reason.

---

*Rev. John A. O'Brien. *The Faith of Millions*, Huntington, Indiana: Our Sunday Visitor Press, 1938, pp. 411–19.

Purgatory and Prayers for the Dead

The Scriptures encourage us to pray not only for one another on earth, and to invoke the intercession of the saints and angels, but they encourage us to pray for the souls of our deceased brethren as well. In the second Book of Machabees it is narrated that after Judas had defeated Gorgias, he came with his company to bury the Jews slain in the battle. "Making a gathering, he sent twelve thousand drachms of silver to Jerusalem for sacrifice to be offered for the sins of the dead." He did not regard their sins to be grievous, "because he considered that they who had fallen asleep with godliness had great grace laid up for them." The sacred writer then expresses the doctrine involved herein: "It is, therefore, a holy and wholesome thought to pray for the dead, that they may be loosed from their sins." (12:43–46)

While our dissenting brethren do not acknowledge the Books of Machabees to be inspired, they must at least admit them to be faithful historical records that bear witness to the Jewish faith centuries before Christ. As a matter of fact, they rest upon the same authority as Isaiah, St. John and all the other books in the Bible—the infallible teaching authority of the Church which has declared all the books in the Bible to be inspired.

Our Savior speaks of the forgiveness of sins in "The world to come" (Matt. 12:32) which refers to Purgatory according to St. Augustine and St. Gregory the Great. In his letter to the Corinthians, St. Paul tells us that "every man's work shall be manifest" on the Lord's day. "The fire" he continues, "shall try every man's work of what sort it is. If any man's work abide," that is, if his works are righteous, "he shall receive a reward. If any man's work burn" this is, if his works are faulty and imperfect, "he shall suffer loss; but he himself shall be saved, yet so as by fire." (I Cor. 3:13–15) In these words St. Paul tells us that the soul of such a man will ultimately be saved, though he will suffer for a time the purifying flames of Purgatory.

This is the unanimous interpretation of the Fathers of the early Church and the continuing tradition of the intervening centuries. It speaks to us from the tombs of the martyrs and from the catacombs where lie the bodies of the early Christians. In going through the catacombs of St. Calixtus under the plain of the Roman campagna outside the walls of Rome, the writer saw a number of inscriptions echoing still the last words of the dying Christians: "In your prayers remember us who have gone before you." "Mayest thou have eternal light in Christ," was the answering prayer of those who remained behind. "Inscriptions such as these," reports Monsignor Barnes, "are found upon the tombs of many Christians in the first three centuries." (*The Early Church in the Light of the Monuments*, 149–157)

This Apostolic custom of praying for the dead is frequently referred to in the writings of the Fathers of both the East and West. Tertullian (160–240) in two different passages speaks of anniversary Masses: "We make on one day every year oblations for the dead, as for their birthdays." (De Cor. Mil., 3) "The faithful widow prays for the soul of her husband, and begs for him in the interim repose, and participation in the first resurrection, and offers prayers on the anniversary of his death." (*De Monag.*, 10)

In his funeral sermon over the Emperor Theodosius, St. Ambrose, Bishop of Milan, said: "Give perfect rest to Thy servant Theodosius, that rest which Thou hast prepared for Thy saints . . . I have loved him, and therefore will I follow him unto the land of the living; nor will I leave him until by tears and prayers I shall lead him whither his merits summon him, unto the holy mountain of the Lord." (*De Obitu. Theod.*, 36, 37)

One of the most touching incidents which have come down to us from the writings of the Fathers upon this subject is from the pen of St. Augustine, who lived in the beginning of the fifth century. This scholarly Bishop relates that when his mother was dying, she made this last request of him: "Lay this body anywhere; let not the care of it in any way disturb you. This only I request of you, that you would remember me at the altar of the Lord, wherever you be." (*Confessions*, Book 9) The memory of that request drew from her son this fervent prayer: "I, therefore, O God of my heart, do now beseech Thee for the sins of my mother. Hear me through the medicine of the wounds that hung upon the wood ... May she, then, be in peace with her husband ... And inspire, my Lord ... thy servants, my brethren, whom with voice and heart and pen I serve, that as many as shall read these words may remember at Thy Altar, Monica, Thy servant ... (*Confessions*, Book 9) In this incident there is reflected the universal custom of the early Church of praying for the dead as well as her belief in a state called *purgatory*.

The custom of offering prayers and sacrifice for the souls of their departed relatives and friends was deeply rooted among the ancient Jews and in spite of all their dispersions and wanderings has continued down to the present day. Some years ago the writer observed great numbers of them praying for their deceased at the famous Wailing Wall in Jerusalem. An authorized prayer-book in common use among the Hebrews in our country contains the following formula of prayers prescribed for funerals:

"Departed brother! mayest thou find open the gates of heaven, and see the city of peace and the dwellings of safety, and meet the ministering angels hastening joyfully toward thee. And may the High Priest stand to receive thee, and go thou to the end, rest in peace, and rise again into life. May the repose established in the celestial abode . . . be the lot, dwelling and the resting-place of the soul of our deceased brother (whom the Spirit of the Lord may guide into Paradise), who departed from this world, according to the will of God, the Lord of heaven and earth. May the supreme King of kings, through His infinite mercy, hide him under the shadow of His wing. May He raise him at the end of his days and cause him to drink of the stream of His delights." (*Jewish Prayer Book.* Edited by Isaac Leeser, Philadelphia: Slote & Mooney)

"It is indeed strange," observes Father B. L. Conway, C.S.P., "that the Reformers should set aside such a body of testimony, both in Scripture and tradition, for Purgatory and prayers for the dead. But doctrine is so interwoven with doctrine in the consistent Gospel of Jesus Christ, that the denial of one central dogma logically means the denial of many others. Luther's false theory of justification by faith alone led him to deny the distinction between mortal and venial sin, the fact of temporal punishment, the necessity of good works, the efficacy of indulgences, and the usefulness of prayers for the dead. If sin is not remitted, but only covered; if the 'new man' of the Gospel is Christ imputing His own justice to the still sinful man, it would indeed be useless to pray for the dead that they be loosed from their sins. Luther's denial of Purgatory implied either the cruel doctrine that the greater number of even devout Christians were lost, which accounts in some measure for the modern denial of eternal punishment, or the unwarranted assumption that God by 'some sudden, magical change' purifies the soul at the instant of death." (*The Question Box,* 395, 396)

While the word *purgatory* does not occur in Scripture, the reality which it symbolizes is referred to both in the Old and the New Testament and in the writing of the Fathers in the East and in the West. Since the belief in the efficacy of prayers for the dead was universal in the infant Church, it follows that the belief in purgatory was likewise universal. For without a purgatory, prayers for the dead would be meaningless.

Purgatory — A Demand of Reason

Entirely aside, however, from the evidence offered by Scripture and tradition, reason alone would suggest and even demand the existence of a midway state between heaven and hell. Since "nothing defiled can enter heaven," it follows that a soul departing this life with either venial sin or with temporal punishment still to be suffered, could not enter heaven. It could not in justice be sent to hell which is everlasting, as such a punishment would be out of all proportion to the offense committed. It is entirely probable that vast numbers of people die with venial sin upon their souls. They are not worthy to enter at once into heaven. They cannot in justice be doomed to hell. There must, therefore, be another state where the punishment is suited to the offense. Such is the imperative dictate of reason. That state which reason thus demands is *purgatory,* where they are cleansed of their venial imperfections and rendered suitable to enter into the august presence of their Lord and Creator in the unspeakable happiness of heaven.

The custom of praying for the souls of our departed friends is not only comformable to Holy Scripture, but is prompted by the instincts of our nature. The doctrine of the communion of saints emphasizes the social and spiritual solidarity of our race by showing how we can help one another in time of need. It goes a long way to rob death of its terrors. In denying this doctrine the Reformers of the sixteenth century did violence not only to the Scriptures and the unbroken tradition of the Christian Church for sixteen centuries, but they halted and jarred also the instincts of our nature and the craving of our hearts. They severed those tender and sacred ties which bind earth with heaven—the soul in the flesh with the soul released from its fleshy tabernacle.

If I may pray for my brother on this earth why may I not continue to pray for him when he has crossed the borderline into eternity? Does not death destroy merely the body, leaving the soul unscathed? Does he not, therefore, still live and think and remember and love? What earthly reason is there then why I should not continue to remember him in my prayers and prove my love for him not by unavailing tears but by the more potent means of my petitions in his behalf addressed to the God of mercy and compassion? What Christian is there who can stand at the open grave and see the body of a loved one being lowered to its resting place without lifting tear-dimmed eyes to heaven with the cry: "O God, have mercy upon the soul of my beloved!"

Regardless of the silence of his Protestant creed upon the efficacy of prayers for the dead, he hearkens to the voice of his heart and responds in that universal language of love and sympathy which all mankind understands. From the mute lips of his deceased friend he hears again the same plea as that uttered by Job in his adversity: "Have pity on me, have pity on me, at least you my friends, because the hand of the Lord hath touched me!" That such an appeal does not fall upon deaf ears is an evidence that the human heart has not allowed religious prejudice to rob it of its love and sympathy. Of souls which have passed beyond the border into eternity and plead to us from purgatory for a remembrance in our prayers we can truly say: "They pass beyond our touch, beyond our sight; never, thank God, beyond our love and prayers."

Out of his long experience of more than fifty years in the ministry, Cardinal Gibbons narrates an incident which illustrates this point: "I have seen," he relates, "a devoted daughter minister with tender solicitude at the sick-bed of a fond parent. Many an anxious day and sleepless night did she watch at his bedside. She moistened the parched lips, and cooled the fevered brow, and raised the drooping head on its pillow. Every change in her patient for better or worse brought a corresponding sunshine or gloom to her heart. It was filial love that prompted all this. Her father died and she followed his remains to the grave. Though not a Catholic, standing by the bier she burst those chains which a cruel religious prejudice had wrought around her heart, and, rising superior to her sect, she cried out: 'Lord, have mercy on his soul.' It was the voice of nature and of religion." (Gibbons, *The Faith of Our Fathers*, p. 224)

Tennyson reflects alike the Christian tradition and the natural yearning of the human heart when he makes his hero, the dying King Arthur, thus address his surviving comrade, Sir Bedivere:

> "I have lived my life, and that which I have done
> May He within Himself make pure; but thou,
> If thou shouldst never see my face again,
> Pray for my soul. More things are wrought by prayer
> Than this world dreams of. Wherefore, let thy voice
> Rise like a fountain for me night and day."

An Appealing Doctrine

When John L. Stoddard was groping in the mists of uncertainty for the sure light of religious truth, he received a letter from a Catholic friend calling his attention to the beauty and reasonableness of the Church's teaching on purgatory. The letter which proved so illuminating and helpful to Stoddard states the case with admirable lucidity as follows: "There is hardly a religious system of antiquity in which some similar provision (to Purgatory) is not found. It was left for the 'Reformers' of the sixteenth century to reject this immemorial dogma of the Church. When they denied the sanctity of the Mass and many other sacramental features of Catholicism, the doctrine of Purgatory went with the rest. If the souls of the dead pass instantly into an eternally fixed state, beyond the efficacy of our intercessions, then all our requiems, prayers and similar practices are vain. But if, on the contrary, we believe in the Communion of Saints, that is, in the intercommunion of the three-fold Church, militant on earth, suffering in Purgatory, and triumphant in Heaven, then we on earth can influence, and be influenced by, the souls who have crossed the border. Few, indeed quit this life in a state of purity and grace which warrants their immediate entrance into Heaven. Still fewer, let us hope, are those to whom the blessed refuge of Purgatory, that half-way house of our dead, is closed. I cannot conceive how Protestants can believe as they do on this point, nor is it astonishing that their rejection of Purgatory has been followed, in the case of many, by the elimination of a belief in Hell; for the latter doctrine, taken alone, is monstrous. In fact, all Catholic doctrines are interdependent; they stand or fall together. You cannot pick stones out of the arch, and expect it to stand, for it will not do so. Purgatory is one of the most humane and beautiful conceptions imaginable. How many mothers' aching hearts has it not soothed and comforted with hope for some dead, wayward son!" (Stoddard, *Rebuilding a Lost Faith,* p. 155)

After his conversion Stoddard wrote the story of his religious wanderings in *Rebuilding a Lost Faith,* in which he thus sets forth the reasonableness of this doctrine which made so powerful an appeal to him: "The doctrine of the Catholic Church in reference to Purgatory states that there is such a place, in which souls suffer for a time, before they can be admitted to the joys of Heaven, because they still need to be cleansed from certain venial sins, infirmities and faults, or still have to discharge the *temporal* punishment due to mortal sins, which is as yet uncancelled, though the *lasting* punishment of those sins has been forgiven and removed through Christ's atonement. Furthermore, the Church declares, that by our prayers and by the acceptable sacrifice of the Mass we may still help those souls, through the merits of Christ. Beyond this statement the Church's formal doctrine does not go; but it is *not* an article of Catholic faith that there is in Purgatory any material fire. It is generally believed that souls in Purgatory suffer spiritual anguish from the fact that they then feel acutely, as they could not do on earth, the perfect happiness from which they are for a time excluded, while they must also understand the enormity of the sins which they committed against their Heavenly Father and their Saviour." (Stoddard, *Rebuilding a Lost Faith,* p. 156)

I have met many Protestants who though they have no doctrine of purgatory in their official creed, acknowledge that they often remember their deceased loved ones in their prayers. I remember a devout Protestant woman who stated that she prayed each day for her son who was killed in an

84

automobile accident a few days after his graduation from the University. Though she had never read a line of St. Augustine, and probably never had heard even his name, yet out of the unquenchable yearning of her heart and the ineradicable instincts of her human nature, she knew his teaching that "there are some who have departed this life, not so bad as to be deemed unworthy of mercy, nor so good as to be entitled to immediate happiness." (*De Civ. Dei.*, 21:24)

In constantly increasing numbers our separated brethren are coming to recognize both the reasonableness and the authentic character, in the light of the teachings of Christ and of the Apostles, of the doctrine of purgatory. As Mallock well observes: "It is becoming fast recognized that it is the only doctrine that can bring a belief in future rewards and punishments into anything like accordance with our notions of what is just and reasonable. So far from its being a superfluous superstition, it is seen to be just what is demanded at once by reason and morality; and a belief in it is not an intellectual assent only, but a partial harmonizing of the whole moral ideal." (*Is Life Worth Living?* p. 290) In short, the doctrine of purgatory answers the demand of reason, harmonizes with the instinctive yearnings of our nature, and reflects the teaching of Christ and His Apostles.

Thoughts on Purgatory*

Perhaps it was the idea of fire which in the Western Church hindered deliberations on purgatory. In order to do away with this impediment, it may suffice to have a discussion on the

---

*The Mystery of Purgatory (Jean Guitton)

official teaching of the Church while at the same time taking into consideration the experiences of the mystics. It is really strange that the topic of purgatory, which should interest all of us—for who has not some friends in this "intermediate state," and who of us knows whether this very evening he may not be there himself—leaves most of the faithful so unconcerned.

I should like to submit here some thoughts which at one and the same time divinize and humanize the idea of purgatory, supposing that these two terms really form a contrast in the religious teaching ("Menschwerdungsreligion") on the Incarnation.

Something which, it seems, most restrains modern man from thinking on the approaching purgatory is his remembering so many writings, so many sermons, so many terrifying stories which describe the tortures suffered by Poor Souls in purgatory. However, until the 19th century, the attitude of most people was such that they did not care when others were tortured. Civil courts of law, and at the time of the Inquisition, even ecclesiastical courts, used the rack. Who could imagine a more sentimental and emotional century than that of Rousseau and Watteau? And yet in that sentimental age people could watch for hours the torturing of the unfortunate Damien who had wounded Louis XV by the stab of a knife.

For us modern people such a thing is simply unbearable. Now the Roman Catholic Church has never determined the nature of atoning suffering in purgatory, and she permits a concept of purgatory which has nothing to do with the idea of physical torture. Death surprises most people in a moment when, on account of their sins and "countless omissions," their spiritual development has not been completed. Therefore, after this life, which on account of man's free will represents a dangerous development, there begins another development, free of any risk or danger, in a different state of existence, during which we become that which in the depths of our souls we have been longing for. There is question here, therefore, of an intermediate state between what we are now and what we shall become.

St. Catherine of Genoa, the mystic of purgatory, makes it very clear that souls, even in the midst of their sufferings, experience great joy. She says in this regard, "The sufferings are so great that no tongue can describe them, no mind can grasp their degree." In some other passage, however, she writes, "I do not believe that anywhere one can find contentment which equals that of the souls in purgatory, unless it be the contentment of the blessed in heaven. This contentment grows day by day, the more God penetrates the soul, and as He penetrates the soul, the more opposing obstacles disappear."

Let us remark here that joy and pain can very well exist side by side. We know from our own experience that sadness may be sweet and joy may be bitter. Dante writes in Canto XXIII of "Purgatorio," this marvelously profound verse:

Domine labia mea aperies per modo
Tale che diletto e doglia parturie.

Who, in moments of greatest joy, has not experienced sadness at the thought of its transitoriness, of the impossibility of sharing it with others, and the realization that it cannot continue as it is? Who does not know of that peace of soul in the midst of some great trial, or that joy over some pain which one knows was sent by God?

Souls who have been favored with mystical experiences know better than all others the mysterious relation between joy and sorrow. The deeper sorrow ploughs, the higher rises the

87

joy out of the furrow. Penitents have told us of the boundless peace they experienced in the midst of the greatest privations. For this reason they almost seek pain, insofar as God permits, by submitting their own will they attain to that happiness which perfect freedom implies.

In analogy with known fact, we shall try to understand the "interior" of the souls in purgatory. The mysterious fire is God, whose presence is indeed felt, but with whom as yet no union is possible. Considering this explanation, purgatory is a state of maturing (perhaps in a single moment, which we, substituting quality by quantity, express in terms of days and years) in which our person is purified by suffering. In this state the change for good, which we could have brought about already during our earthly life, is continued. However, now in this state there is no longer danger of not making use of opportunities. The term "torture" should designate only that pain which is caused by remorse of conscience; other pains do not deserve this name as they are accompanied by a joy which otherwise is known only to the saints. And how beautiful in its humble expectation is that last word of Mr. de Saci, handed down to us by Sainte-Beuve, "O blessed purgatory!"

In accordance with our imperfect nature, we assess the duration of purgatory in terms of human ideas of time. Nevertheless our reason tells us that there obviously is question of some other kind of time, of a time of unhampered progress, of purification without torment, of suffering without revolt, of a spiritual time, of a time of pure, refining development. It must be a time like the one through which a soul passes when severe trials are willingly accepted, a time which despoils nothing but rather rectifies everything, a time weighed down neither by thoughts of a terrible past nor by fear of the future, because every moment glides over into a more beautiful one, every moment brings a greater certainty of eternal salvation.

We know from our own experience that there are two ways of bearing sufferings. When some severe trial befalls us, we can accept it willingly, knowing that it serves our purification. This is the earthly comparison of the sufferings of the "catharsis" experienced in purgatory. On the other hand one can envelop himself in his sufferings, can rebel and protest. By this rebellion pain becomes a torment. Sufferings in purgatory are of the first kind. Hell, however, is that rebellious kind of suffering, wrapped up in itself, for which there is no relief.

The three states which we call heaven, purgatory and hell, rest on the principle of eternal love. Where there is no obstacle to this love, it appears as pure light and brings perfect joy. Where some obstacle appears, this love appears as fire, of which there are two kinds. In the first case, purgatory, the obstacle is of a passive nature, so to speak, a rheumatism of the soul, an illness, a feebleness. In the second case there is active resistance which dominates the soul, assents to what is evil, and rebels. Purgatory is a fire of joyous celebration; the fire of hell is one of torment. Love always enfolds us; it lies with us to choose to change it into fire or into light.

From all this we can understand that a very peculiar and deep mysticism may inspire those persons who dedicate themselves to helping the Poor Souls. There is then question not only of a kind of visiting the imprisoned, though this idea of charity and compassion need not be absolutely excluded. How should He who called those blessed who visit His sick and suffering members not also bless the visits that we make, in reverent thought and prayer, to the mysterious place of retention and of purification in light?

However, there are still other aspects. The souls in purgatory participate in experiences which are similar to those of the great mystics and even of the Mother of God, although sin was unknown to her. However, unlike the greatest mystics on earth who still have to struggle and whose end is still somewhat uncertain, thè Poor Souls are free of any unrest and anxiety. They are in the hand of God; they have been saved. It is true, the long waiting for their release will cause them pain, which may be the greater the nearer they approach their deliverance. At least I myself had this experience as a prisoner of war. The Poor Souls have this one, absolute certainty: they are in eternity and on the right side of eternity. They no longer experience what Cardinal Newman in "The Dream of Gerontius," that wonderful poem on paradise, calls, "the busy beat of time." They have been freed of their mortal body and their social obligations. Therefore, they belong entirely to God; they are entirely in God; they are entirely for God. It is even possible that they themselves do not wish for an abbreviation of this time of painful waiting if that would mean a lower degree of eternal happiness.

We, therefore, can understand when contemplative persons unite themselves with them. They help them and are themselves helped by them. There occurs between them an interchange of joy, sorrow, and love. They form a community with earthly and heavenly values. Among the many possibilities offered to the human mind for uniting what is visible with what is invisible, and what belongs to time with what belongs to eternity, this one is perhaps the most concrete, the most efficacious, the most human; I almost said, the most joyous. And why should I not say that? Whoever met people who had made it their special concern to pray for and with the Souls in

Purgatory, must have noticed that a certain bliss radiates from them.

This makes us conclude that, in spite of the torment of purgatory, there is in the midst of this intermediate stage an ocean of peace and serenity. And for us poor sinful humans, who hardly can hope to be immediately admitted to the blissful vision of God, it is a joy to know that also in this place of purgation we shall find again the tender bonds of friendship which we had enjoyed on earth. The family is not torn asunder, but arises anew in the eternal mansions. The separation through death, on one hand, and that between purgatory and heaven, on the other hand, is a separation between loving persons. It causes a multiplication of their loving relationship and a growth of love.

—Jean Guitton

One should not reject from the outset the thought that God can permit a soul, in the moment when it is leaving the body, or a Poor Soul from purgatory, to make some kind of impression upon living persons. When God permits a soul from the other world to speak to one in this world, He does it always with holy designs concerning salvation. He wants by such extraordinary means to sanctify that soul—not to satisfy human curiosity or arouse fear and terror.

—Dr. J. Klug. *Der Katholische Glaubensinhalt*

It is certain that without God's willing it, the Poor Souls can never, not even temporarily, leave the abode to which they have been assigned. But it is also certain that God's goodness and mercy is great enough to permit a departed soul a tempor-

ary absence and make its appearing possible either for its own consolation or for the good of someone still in this world. . . .
—Prof. Dr. Kaulen in *Wetzer und Weltes Kirchenlexikon*

What Does The Catechism Teach Us About Purgatory?

How marvellous must heaven be if God exacts such a painfully strict purification of the souls.
—St. Catherine of Siena

Whoever dies in the state of grace, but has not yet been purified of all sins and punishment for sins, cannot immediately enter heaven. St. John writes, concerning the heavenly Jerusalem, "Nothing unclean may come into it." (Rev. 21:27) Whoever, therefore, has still to atone for sins or make up for punishment for sins must first enter a place of purgation, which we call purgatory.

The Poor Souls are filled with bitter sorrow for their sins and with a burning longing for the good and holy God. They have to expiate their punishment for sins by great sufferings. The greatest of them is to be excluded from the blissful vision of God; their greatest consolation is the certainty that they will see Him soon and that they have been saved for all eternity.

The Poor Souls themselves can do nothing to shorten their sufferings. But Jesus Christ, their divine Savior, incessantly makes intercession for them with the Father, and, through Him, also the Blessed Virgin and the other saints of heaven. We, too, through Jesus Christ, can pray and make sacrifices for the Poor Souls that they may quickly be released from their sufferings.

Purgatory will last until the Last Judgment. After the Last Judgment there will be only heaven and hell.

—Cited from the German General Catechism, page 255.

Apparitions of Poor Souls to Some Saints

Following are four examples as proof that well known saints also had apparitions of Poor Souls.

Margaret Mary Alacoque (1647–1690) writes in her autobiography:

"On one occasion, when I was praying before the Blessed Sacrament on the Feast of Corpus Christi, a figure suddenly appeared before me, completely enveloped in flames, the heat of which penetrated me so powerfully that I believed myself to be burning as well. The pitiful condition in which I beheld that soul caused me to shed abundant tears. He told me that he was a Benedictine monk to whom I once went to confession and who had exhorted me to receive Holy Communion. For this reason Our Lord allowed him to have recourse to me that he might obtain some alleviation in his sufferings. He asked me to apply to his soul all that I should do and suffer for three months, which I promised with the consent of my superior . . . At the expiration of the three months I saw him again, resplendent with joy, being about to be admitted to eternal bliss. He thanked me and promised to be my intercessor before God.

John Bosco (1815–1888). In 1839 John Bosco lost his best friend, Luigi Comollo. The two young friends had audaciously agreed to the following: Whoever died first was to return to the survivor to put him at peace concerning his fate in the other world. During the night following the funeral, suddenly a horrible din arose in the dormitory where about 20 seminarians were sleeping. Fires flashed on and off. The house trembled. A voice was heard, "I am saved!" The seminarians were terribly frightened; nobody dared to stir before daybreak. An incredible story! However, all witnesses testified to the truth of it.

St. Gertrude the Great (+ about 1302) was abbess at Helfta and authoress of the famous, *Ambassador of Divine Love.* She once saw the soul of a deceased nun who showed by her demeanor that she did not dare approach her divine bridegroom. When asked for the reason, she answered, "Because I have not yet been perfectly cleansed from the stains of my sins. Even if Jesus would offer me in this condition free entrance into heaven, I would not accept, for though I appear radiantly beautiful in your eyes, I know very well that I am not a worthy spouse of my Lord."

St. Christina of Belgium, a shepherd girl of St. Trond, diocese of Liege, was also called Christina Mirabilis because of the marvelous happenings in her life as testified to by eye witnesses. She was allowed to see heaven and purgatory in a vision. "Christina," she heard a voice saying to her, "You are now in the bliss of heaven. You have the choice of remaining forever in the midst of the elect, or returning for some more years to earth in order to help the Poor Souls by good works. If you choose the former, you will be safe and have nothing more to fear. In the other case, you will return to earth to suffer a real martyrdom, help the wretched ones, and beautify your heavenly crown . . ." Christina answered, "Lord, let me return to suffer for the deceased souls. I fear no pain, no bitterness."

Saint Brigitta, a noble woman of Sweden, who died in 1373 in Rome, writes, "Just as a hungry person welcomes food; a thirsty one, drink; a naked one, clothing; and a sick one the bed in which he is laid, so the Poor Souls welcome and receive the good that is done for them in this world."

Museum of the Souls in Purgatory in Rome

Father Reginald-Omez, O.P., writes in his book, *Kann Man Mit Den Toten in Verbindung Treten? (Can One Communicate with the Poor Souls?):* Several times we visited the famous Museum of the Souls in Purgatory in Rome. The museum was established in 1900 by Father Victor Jouet, priest of the Sacred Heart, and founder of the magazine, PURGATORY. In this museum visitors will find a strange and unique collection.

There one can see burn marks which are said to have been produced by the Poor Souls. They are, for instance, on prayer books (as on the one which belonged to Margarete Dammerle of Erlingen); on missals; on clothing (as on the shirt of Sieur Joseph Leleux of Mons, which has an impression of burning fingers, and is dated January 21, 1789). There is also the badly scorched military cloak of an Italian sentinel who one night in 1932 had to guard, in the Pantheon, the sepulcher of the murdered King Humbert I, whose ghost pressed a fiery hand on the shoulder of the guard after having given him a message for King Victor Emmanuel III.

One can also see a cross, perfectly drawn with the tip of a red-hot forefinger. Conceding that such impressions are not the effect of chance or of conscious fraud, it is in any case clear that they cannot have been caused by means of the spiritual fire which has seized the departed souls. They can only be the effect of a miracle wrought by God who for this purpose created an element capable of scorching these objects and leaving on them the black scar which is a symbol of the spiritual burning of souls in the state of expiation.

Citations and Prayers

Those souls who belong to the suffering Church usually appear to the living in a form and attitude which arouse the compassion of those who see them . . . always, however, at the sight of such a material sign, there comes to our mind the thought of some person especially dear to us, and we feel stimulated to pray for that person.

—Scaramelli, *Voss. Direct. Mystic.* Compendium 1, i.

Our united prayer should rise daily to heaven for all the members of the Mystical Body of Jesus Christ . . . No member of this venerated body must be forgotten in this common prayer; and let there be a special remembrance for the suffering souls in purgatory.

—Pius XII, in *Mystici Corporis*

Love embraces also those who have died in this love, for love is the life of the soul just as the soul is the life of the body.

—St. Thomas Aquinas

Although purgatory is a chastisement, it is at the same time a remedy. We shall easily understand this if we think a little on what sin does to a person. Sin is poison for the soul. It is true, absolution takes away the sin, but it cannot take away the effect which the poison had on the soul; its life has been weakened.

Sin wounds the soul. Even if the wound has healed, a scar remains.

Sin is the sickness of the soul; to cure it requires sacrifice.

Every supernatural damage must be repaired by supernatural means, either in this world or in the other.

—Andrée Bourcois-Macé

Jesus Christ has deigned to call the Church His spouse and He calls the unbroken unity of the faithful His body, whose divine head He is Himself. Now it is certain that the part of this body which is suffering most are the holy souls in purgatory. Nowhere on this earth can be found suffering that would equal their martyrdom. Don't you believe, then, that when Jesus sees in your heart a special, great compassion with these suffering souls, He will also give you a special, great share in His love?

—Etienne Binet, S.J., in his work on purgatory (17th Century)

As love is the bond which unites the members of the Church with one another, it embraces the living as well as those who have departed this life in that love. Due to this love, therefore, the sacrifice of the faithful can aid the departed members.

—Denis, the Carthusian

Romano Guardini once wrote that little could be said about the other world if the life of man could be divided simply into good and evil. But man is a complex being in whom good and evil are found so close together that often it is difficult to separate them from one another (consider, for instance, Christ's parable of the wheat and the cockle).

The human being is God's most beautiful creature. God wanted to unite himself with him to find his pleasure in Him. This being He has destined for perfect union with Himself. If, therefore, this creature has been freed from all earthly material bonds and appears before Him, He wants to see it clothed in perfection, absolutely worthy of His love.

—J. M. Szymusiak, S.J.

Wake up, you sleepers;
Pray to God for the Poor Souls!
—Call of the night watchman in former times, in the towns and villages of France

If people would know how great is the power of these good departed souls over the heart of God, and if they would know how abundant are the graces we can obtain through their intercession, the Poor Souls would not be so forgotten. You must pray much for them; then they will pray much for you.

—St. John Vianney, Curé of Ars

We live of the goods our ancestors and parents have acquired and yet so easily we forget what we owe to them and how ardently they long for our gratitude, needing our help. They call out, "Be patient, suffer, pray, fast, give alms for us! Offer the Holy Sacrifice of the Mass for us!"

—Anna Katherine Emmerich, Augustinian nun

Fire will test the quality of each man's work.

—Paul, Cor. 3:13

How happy we are that we ended our lives in peace with God, but here he makes us suffer through our longing to see Him.

—Dante, *Purgatorium*, 36

Patron of the Poor Souls

"This only I request, that you would remember me at the Lord's altar, wherever you may be."

—Request of St. Monica to Augustine

Beside the Archangel Michael, the patron of the Poor Souls is St. Odilo (962–1048). When he was still a young man, he renounced great estates and became a monk. As abbot of Cluny he became the great reformer and organizer of the monasticism of his time. His guiding principle was, "I would rather be judged by God for too great leniency than for too great severity."

In 1016, when a great famine broke out, he had all the supplies of the monastery distributed; he even sold church vessels in order to distribute more bread. He used to say, "Since Christ shed His blood for us, we may not withhold anything from the poor."

We owe to him the introduction of the commemoration of All Souls' Day.

Psalm 130 – *De Profundis*

Out of the depths I cry to you, O Lord,
   Lord, hear my voice!

O let your ears be attentive
  to the voice of my pleading.
If you, O Lord, should mark our guilt,
  Lord, who would survive?
But with you is found forgiveness:
  for this we revere you.
My soul is waiting for the Lord,
  I count on his word.
My soul is longing for the Lord
  more than watchmen for daybreak.
Let the watchmen count on daybreak
  and Israel on the Lord.
Because with the Lord there is mercy
  and fulness of redemption,
Israel indeed he will redeem
  from all its iniquity.
*Eternal Rest Grant Unto Them, O Lord, And Let Perpetual
Light Shine Upon Them. May They Rest in Peace.   Amen.*

God cannot change his essence. Holiness is his being. Holy
he must be ever. But because he is holy, no unholy soul can
attain to the blissful happiness of heaven.

—Cardinal John Henry Newman

Like the deer that yearns for running streams, so my soul
  is yearning for you, my God.
My soul is thirsting for God, the God of my life;
  when can I enter and see the face of God?

—Psalm 42:2–3

O Jesus, victim of love, make me a living sacrifice for Thee, holy, pleasing unto God.

—Ejaculatory prayer of St. Pope Pius X

Authorized translation:
Father, all-powerful and ever-living God, we do well always and everywhere to give you thanks through Jesus Christ our Lord. In him, who rose from the dead, our hope of resurrection dawned. The sadness of death gives way to the bright promise of immortality. Lord, for your faithful people life is changed, not ended. When the body of our earthly dwelling lies in death we gain an everlasting dwelling place in heaven. And so, with all the choirs of angels in heaven, we proclaim your glory and join in their unending hymn of praise.

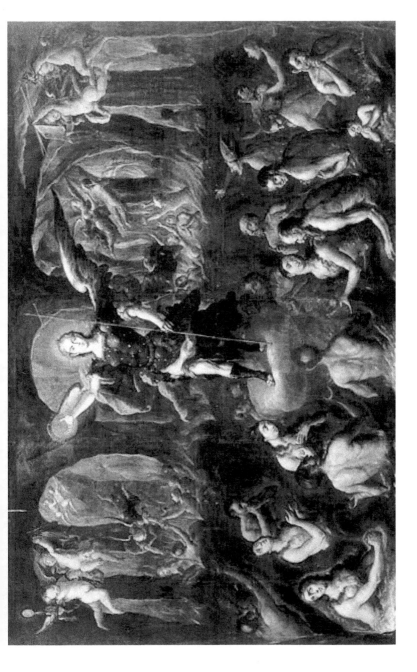

BUTLER'S LIVES OF THE SAINTS

NOVEMBER II

ALL SOULS; OR, THE COMMEMORATION OF THE FAITHFUL DEPARTED

By PURGATORY, no more is meant by Catholics than a middle state of souls, viz. Of purgation from sin by temporary
chastisements, or a punishment of some sin inflicted after
death, which is not eternal.[*] As to the place, manner, or
kind of these sufferings, nothing has been defined by the
church; and all who with Dr. Deacon except against this
doctrine, on account of the circumstance of a material
fire,[†] quarrel about a mere scholastic question in which a
person is at liberty to choose either side. This doctrine of a
state of temporary punishment after death for some sins, is
interwoven with the fundamental articles of the Christian
religion. For, as eternal torments are the portion of all souls
which depart this life under the guilt of mortal sin, and everlasting bliss of those who die in the state of grace, so it is
an obvious consequence that among the latter, many souls
may be defiled with lesser stains, and cannot enter immediately into the joy of the Lord. Repentance may be sincere, though something be wanting to its perfection; some
part of the debt which the penitent owes to the Divine

---

[*] See the Council of Trent, Sess. 25; Pope Pius IV's Creed, Bossuet's
Exposition, and Catech. of Montp.
[†] Deacon, Tr. on Purgatory.

Justice may remain uncancelled, as appears from several instances mentioned in the holy scriptures, as of David,[*] of the Israelites in the wilderness,[†] of Moses and Aaron,[‡] and of the prophet slain by a lion,[§] which debt is to be satisfied for, either in this life or in the next. Certainly, some sins are venial, which deserve not eternal death; yet if not effaced by condign penance in this world, must be punished in the next. Every wound is not mortal; nor does every small offence totally destroy friendship. The scriptures frequently mention these venial sins, from which ordinarily the just are not exempt, who certainly would not be just if these lesser sins into which men easily fall by surprise, destroyed grace in them, or if they fell from charity.[¶] Yet the smallest sin excludes a soul from heaven so long as it is not blotted out. Nothing which is not perfectly pure and spotless can stand before God, who is infinite purity and sanctity, and cannot bear the sight of the least iniquity. Whence it is said of heaven: *There shall in no wise enter into it any thing defiled.*[**] It is the great employment of all the saints or pious persons here below by rigorous self-examination to try their actions and thoughts, and narrowly to look into all the doublings and recesses of their hearts; continually to accuse and judge themselves, and by daily tears of compunction, works of penance, and the use of the sacraments, to correct all secret disorders, and wipe away all filth which their affections may contract. Yet who is there who keeps so constant a guard upon his heart and whole conduct as to avoid all insensible self-deceptions? Who is

---

* 2 Kings (or Samuel) xiv. 10, and 13, ib. xxiv.
† Num. xiv. 20.
‡ Num. xx. 24; Deut. xxxii. 51.
§ 3 Kings (or 1 Kings) xiii.
¶ Prov. xiv. 16; James iii, 2; Matt. xii. 36; Matt. vi. 12.
** Apoc. xxi. 27.

there upon whose heart no inordinate attachments steal; into whose actions no sloth, remissness, or some other irregularity ever insinuates itself? Or whose compunction and penance is so humble and clear-sighted, so fervent and perfect, that no lurking disorder of his whole life escapes him, and is not perfectly washed away by the sacred blood of Christ, applied by these means or conditions to the soul? Who has perfectly subdued and regulated all his passions, and grounded his heart in perfect humility, meekness, charity, piety, and all other virtues, so as to bear the image of God in himself, or to be holy and perfect even as he is, without spot? Perhaps scarce in any moment of our lives is our intention or motive so fervent, and so pure or exempt from the least imperceptible sinister influence and mixture of sloth, self-complacency, or other inordinate affection or passion; and all other ingredients or circumstances of our action so perfect and holy, as to be entirely without failure in the eyes of God, which nothing can escape. Assiduous conversation with heaven, constant watchfulness, self-denial, and a great purity of heart, with the assistance of an extraordinary grace, give the saints a wonderful light to discover and correct the irregularities of their affections. Yet it is only by the fervent spirit and practice of penance that they can be purified in the sight of God.

The Blessed Virgin was preserved by an extraordinary grace from the least sin in the whole tenor of her life and actions; but, without such a singular privilege, even the saints are obliged to say that they sin daily; but they forthwith rise again by living in constant compunction and watchfulness over themselves.* Venial sins of surprise are readily effaced by penance, as we hope of the divine mercy:

---

* Prov. xxiv. 16.

FR. ALBAN BUTLER

even such sins which are not discovered by us, are virtually repented of by a sincere compunction, if it be such as effectually destroys them. Venial sins of malice, or committed with full deliberation, are of a different nature, far more grievous and fatal, usually of habit, and lead even to mortal sin. Those Christians who shun these more wilful offences, yet are not very watchful over themselves, and labor not very strenuously in subduing all their passions, have just reason to fear that some inordinate affections taint almost the whole body of their actions, without being sufficiently repented of. And the very best Christians must always tremble at the thought of the dreadful account they have to give to God for every idle word or thought. No one can be justified before God but by his pure and free mercy. But how few even among fervent Christians bring, by his grace, the necessary conditions of cleanness and disengagement of heart and penance, in so perfect a manner as to obtain such a mercy, that no blemishes or spots remain in their souls? Hence a saint prayed: *Enter not into judgment with thy servant; for in thy sight shall no man living be justified.*[*] No soul which leaves this world defiled with the least stain, or charged with the least debt to the Divine Justice, can be admitted in the kingdom of perfect purity and unspotted sanctity, till she be perfectly purged and purified. Yet no man will say, that a venial sin which destroys not sanctifying grace, will be punished with eternal orments. Hence there must be a relaxation of some sin in the world to come, as is sufficiently implied, according to the remark of St. Austin, in these words of Christ where he says, that the sin against the Holy Ghost *shall not be forgiven in this world, nor in the world to*

* Psalm cxliii. 2.

come.[*] Christ, exhorting us to agree with our adversary or accuser by appeasing our conscience, mentions a place of punishment out of which souls shall be delivered, though not before they shall have paid the last farthing.[†] St. Paul tells us,[‡] that he whose work shall abide the trial, shall be rewarded; but he who shall have built upon the foundation (which is Christ or his sanctifying grace) wood, hay, or stubble, or whose imperfect and defective works shall not be able to stand the fiery trial, shall be saved, yet so as by fire. The last sentence in the general judgment only mentions heaven and hell, which are the two great receptacles of all men, both the good and bad, for eternity, and after the last judgment there will be no purgatory. It is also very true of every man at his death that on whatever side the tree falls, on that it shall always lie; the doom of the soul is then fixed forever either to life or death: but this excludes not a temporary state of purgation before the last judgment, through which some souls enter into everlasting life. This doctrine of a purgatory will be more evidently proved from the following demonstration of the Catholic practice of praying for the souls of the faithful departed.

The Church of Christ is composed of three different parts: the Triumphant in heaven, the Militant on earth, and the patient or suffering in purgatory. Our charity embraces all the members of Christ. Our love for him engages and binds us to his whole body, and teaches us to share both the miseries and afflictions, and the comforts and blessings of all that are comprised in it. The communion of saints which we profess in our Creed implies a communication of certain good works and offices, and a mutual intercourse

---

[*] Matt. xii. 32, S. Aug. l. 21, De Civ. Dei, c. 13.
[†] Matt. v. 27.
[‡] 1 Cor. iii. 13. On these texts see the Catechism of Montpellier, t. 2, p. 342, ed Latinæ.

among all the members of Christ. This we maintain with the saints in heaven by thanking and praising God for their triumphs and crowns, imploring their intercession, and receiving the succors of their charitable solicitude and prayers for us: likewise with the souls in purgatory, by soliciting the divine mercy in their favor. Nor does it seem to be doubted but they, as they are in a state of grace and charity, pray also for us; though the church never addresses public suffrages to them, not being warranted by primitive practice and tradition so to do. That to pray for the faithful departed is a pious and wholesome charity and devotion, is proved clearly from the Old Testament, and from the doctrine and practice of the Jewish synagogue. The baptisms or legal purifications which the Jews sometimes used for the dead, demonstrate their belief that the dead receive spiritual succors from the devotion of the living.[*] In the second book of the Machabees[†] it is related, that Judas the Machabee sent twelve thousand drachms of silver to the temple for sacrifices to be offered for the dead, *thinking well and religiously concerning the resurrection.—It is therefore a holy and a wholesome thought to pray for the dead, that they may be loosed from their sins.* This book is ranked among the canonical scriptures by the Apostolical Canons, Tertullian, St. Cyprian, St. Hilary, St. Ambrose, St. Austin, the third council of Carthage, &c. Some ancients call it apocryphal, meaning that it was not in the Hebrew canon compiled by Esdras, it being written after his time: and Origen and St. Jerom, who give it that epithet, sometimes quoted it as of divine authority. The Catholic church admits the deutero-canonical books of those which were compiled after the time of

---

[*] 1 Cor. xv. 29; Ecclus. vii. 27.
[†] 2. Mac. xii. 43, 46.

Esdras, as written equally by divine inspiration. If some among the ancients doubted of them before tradition in this point had been examined and cleared, several parts of the New Testament which are admitted by Protestants, have been no less called in question. Protestants, who at least allow this book an historical credit, must acknowledge this to have been the belief and practice of the most virtuous and zealous high-priest, of all the priests and doctors attached to the service of the temple, and of the whole Jewish nation: and a belief and custom which our Blessed Redeemer nowhere reprehended in them. Whence the learned Protestant, Dr. Jeremy Taylor, writes thus:* "We find by the history of the Machabees, that the Jews did pray and make offerings for the dead, which appears by other testimonies, and by their form of prayer still extant, which they used in the captivity. Now it is very considerable, that since our Blessed Saviour did reprove all the evil doctrines and traditions of the Scribes and Pharisees, and did argue concerning the dead and the resurrection, yet he spake no word against this public practice, but left it as he found it; which he who came to declare to us all the will of his Father, would not have done, if it had not been innocent, pious, and full of charity. The practice of it was at first, and was universal: it being plain in Tertullian and St. Cyprian," &c.

The faith and practice of the Christian church from the beginning is manifest from the writings of the primitive fathers. In all ancient liturgies (or masses) express mention is made of prayer and sacrifice for the dead.† St. Cyril of Jerusalem, expounding to the catechumens the several

---

* Dr. Jer. Taylor, Lib. of Proph. l. 1, sect. 20, n. 11, p. 345.
† Beausobre, in his History of Manicheism, (l. 9, c. 3, not.) pretends that St. Cyril of Jerusalem had altered the liturgy on this article; but he is solidly refuted by the learned Henry a Porta, professor at Pavis, Append. ad tractat de Purgat. Mediolani, 1758.

parts of the liturgy, says,[*] that in it we pray for the emperor and all the living: we also name the martyrs and saints to commend ourselves to their prayers; then mention the faithful departed to pray for them. "We remember," says he, "those that are deceased, first the patriarchs, apostles, and martyrs, that God would receive our supplications through their prayers and intercession. Then we pray for our fathers and bishops, and in general for all among us who are departed this life, believing that this will be the greatest relief to them for whom it is made while the holy and tremendous victim lies present." These words of this father are quoted by Eustratius, in the sixth age, and by Nico the Monk.[†] St. Cyril goes on, and illustrates the efficacy of such a prayer by the comparison of a whole nation which, in a joint body, should address their king in favor of persons whom he should have banished, offering him at the same time a crown. "Will not he," says the father, "grant them a remission of their banishment? In like manner, we, offering our prayers for the dead, though they are sinners, offer not a crown, but Christ sacrificed for our sins, studying to render the merciful God propitious to us and to them." Arnobius, speaking of our public liturgies, says:[‡] "In which peace and pardon are begged of God for kings, magistrates, friends and enemies, both the living and those who are delivered from the body." In the Apostolical Constitutions is extant a very ancient fragment of a liturgy, from which Grabe, Hicks, and Deacon borrow many things for their new models of primitive liturgies, and which Whiston pretended to rank among the canonical scriptures. In it occurs a prayer for the dead: "Let us pray for

* Catech. 19, n. 9, p. 328, ed. Ben.
† See the notes of the Benedictins, ibid.
‡ L. 4, adversus Gentes.

those who are departed in peace."* There is no liturgy used by any sect of Oriental Christians, though some have been separated from the communion of the church ever since the fifth or sixth centuries, in which prayer for the dead does not occur.† The most ancient fathers frequently speak of the offering the holy sacrifice of the altar for the faithful departed. Tertullian, the oldest among the Latin Christian writers, mentioning certain apostolical traditions, says: "We make yearly offerings (or sacrifices) for the dead, and for the feasts of the martyrs."‡ He says, "that a widow prays for the soul of her deceased husband, and begs repose for him, and his company in the first resurrection, and offers (sacrifice) on the anniversary days of his death. For if she does not these things, she has, as much as lies in her, divorced him."§ St. Cyprian mentions the usual custom of celebrating sacrifice for every deceased Christian.¶ Nor can it be said that he speaks in the same manner of martyrs. The distinction he makes is evident:** "It is one thing to be cast into prison not to be released till the last farthing is paid, and another thing through the ardor of faith, immediately to attain to the reward: it is very different by long punishment for sin to be cleansed a long time by fire, and to have purged away all sin by suffering." St. Chrysostom reckons it amongst the dreadful obligations of a priest, "that he is the intercessor to God for the sins both of the living and the dead."†† In another place he says: "It is not in vain that in the divine mysteries we remember the dead, appearing in their behalf, praying the Lamb who has taken away the

---

* Constit. Apost. l. 8, c. 13.
† See Le Brun, Litur.
‡ L. de Cor. c. 3.
§ L. de Monog. c. 10.
¶ Ep. 1, Ed. Oxon. See Fleury, t. 2, p. 273.
** Ep. Cypr. ep. ad Antonian. Pam. et Baluzio 52, Fello 55.
†† De Sacerd. l. 6, p. 424, ed. Montfaucon.

sins of the world, that comfort may thence be derived upon them. He who stands at the altar, cries not out in vain: Let us pray for them who have slept in Christ. Let us not fail to succor the departed: for the common expiation of the world is offered."[*] The Protestant translators of Du Pin observe, that St. Chrysostom, in his thirty-eighth homily on the Philippians, says, that to pray for the faithful departed in the tremendous mysteries was decreed by the apostles.[†] Mr. Thorndike, a Protestant theologian, says:[‡] "The practice of the church of interceding for the dead at the celebration of the eucharist, is so general and so ancient, that it cannot be thought to have come in upon imposture, but that the same aspersion will seem to take hold of the common Christianity." Prayer for the faithful departed is mentioned by the fathers on other occasions. St. Clement of Alexandria, who flourished in the year 200, says, that by punishment after death men must expiate every the least sin, before they can enter heaven.[§] The vision of St. Perpetua is related by St. Austin, and in her acts.[¶] Origen in many places,[**] and Lactantius,[††] teach at large, that all souls are purged by the punishment of fire before they enter into bliss, unless they are so pure as not to stand in need of it.

To omit others, St. Austin expounds those words of the thirty-seventh psalm, *Rebuke me not in thy fury*, of hell; and those which follow: *Neither chastise me in thy wrath,* of purgatory, as follows: "That you purify me in

---

* Hom. 51, in 1 Cor. t. 10, p. 393.
† Du Pin, Cent. 3, ed. Angl.: S. Chrys. hom. 3, in Phil. t. 11, p. 217, ed. Mont.
‡ Just Weights and Measures, c. 16, p. 106.
§ Strom. l. 7, p. 794, 865.
¶ See S. Aug. Serm. 280, p. 1134, her Life, 7. March, and Orsi Diss. de Actis SS. Perpet. et Felicit.
** 5, contra Cels. p. 242, Hom. 28, in Num. Hom. 6, et 8, in Exod. &c.
†† Lactant. l. 7, Instit. c. 21.

this life, and render me such that I may not stand in need of that purging fire."* In his Enchiridion,† he says: "Nor is it to be denied that the souls of the departed are relieved by the piety of their living friends, when the sacrifice of the Mediator is offered for them, or alms are given in the church. But these things are profitable to those who, while they lived, deserved that they might avail them.—There is a life so good as not to require them; and there is another so wicked, that after death it can receive no benefit from them. When, therefore, the sacrifices of the altar or alms are offered for all Christians, for the very good they are thanksgivings; they are propitiations for those who are not very bad. For the very wicked, they are some kind of comfort to the living." This father teaches that a funeral pomp and monument are comforts of the living, but no succor of the dead; but that prayer, sacrifices, and alms, relieve the departed.‡ He repeats often that sacrifice is offered in thanksgiving to God for martyrs, but never for their repose. "It is an injury," says he, "to pray for a martyr, to whose prayers we ought to be ourselves recommend-ed."§ And again: "You know in what place (of the liturgy) the martyrs are named. The church prays not for them. She justly prays for other deceased persons, but prays not for the martyrs, but rather recommends herself to their prayers." This he often repeats in other places. St. Austin,¶ and St. Epiphanius,** relate, that when Aërius, an impious

* S. Aug. in Ps. 37, n. 3, p. 295.
† Enchir. c. 110, De Civ. Dei, l. 21, c. 24, l. de Curâ pro Mortuis, c. 4, et serm. 182, (ol. 32.) de verb, ap., where he says that prayer for the dead in the holy mysteries was observed by the whole church.
‡ Serm. 182, (ol. 32.) de verb. ap. t. 5, p. 827, et 1, de Curâ pro Mortuis, c. 1, et 18.
§ Serm. 159, fol. 17, de verb. ap. n. 1, t. 5, p. 765, ed. Ben.; Serm. 284, p. 1143.
¶ S. Aug. l. de hæres, c. 53.
** S. Epiph. hær. 75, n. 3.

Arian priest, denied suffrages for the dead, this heresy was condemned by the universal church. How earnestly St. Monica on her death-bed begged the sacrifices and prayers of the church after her departure, and how warmly St. Austin recommended the souls of his parents to the prayers of others is related in their lives.[*]

The like earnest desire we discover in all ancient Christians and saints. St. Ephrem, in his testament, entreats his friends to offer for him, after his departure, alms, prayers, and oblations, (or masses,) especially on the thirtieth day.[†] St. Athanasius tells Constantius, that he had prayed earnestly for the soul of that emperor's deceased brother, Constans.[‡] Eusebius relates,[§] that Constantine the Great would be buried in the porch of the church of the apostles, "that he might enjoy the communication of the holy prayers, the mystical sacrifice, and the divine ceremonies." The same historian testifies[¶] that after his death, "numberless multitudes poured forth prayers to God with sighs and tears for the soul of the emperor, repaying a most grateful office to their pious prince. St. Paulinus upon his brother's death wrote to his friends, earnestly recommending him to their prayers, that by them his poor soul amidst scorching flames might receive the dew of refreshment and comfort.[**] St. Ambrose, writing to one Faustinus, who grieved immoderately for the death of his sister, says: "I do not think your sister ought to excite your tears, but your prayers: nor that her soul is to be dishonored by weeping, but rather recommended

[*] Conf. l. 9, c. 13, n. 36, &c.
[†] T. 2, ed. Vatic. p. 230, 236.
[‡] S. Athan. Apol. ad Constant., t. 1, p. 300.
[§] De Vitâ Const. l. 4, c. 60, p. 556, et e. 70, p. 562.
[¶] Ib. c. 71, p. 562.
[**] S. Paulin. ep. 35, ad Delfin. p. 223, ep. 36, ad Amand. p. 224, &c.

to God by sacrifices."* In his funeral oration on the great Theodosius he prays thus: "Give perfect rest to thy servant Theodosius."† And again: "I loved him, therefore I follow him unto the country of the living. Neither will I forsake him till by tears and prayers I shall bring the man whither his merits call him, unto the holy mountain of the Lord."‡ He mentions the most solemn obsequies and sacrifices on the thirtieth, sometimes fortieth day;§ for so long they were continued; but, on third, seventh, and thirtieth days, with particular solemnity.¶ St. Gregory the Great mentions that he having ordered thirty masses to be sung for a monk named Justus, on the thirtieth day after the last mass was said, Justus appeared to Copiosus his provos and said: "I was in pain, but now am well."

It appears from Ven. Bede's history, and the account of his death,** also from a great number of letters of St. Boniface, St. Lullus,†† and others, how earnest and careful our ancestors were, from their conversion to the faith, in mutually desiring and offering sacrifices and prayers for their deceased brethren, even in distant countries. In the foundations of churches monasteries, and colleges, in pious instruments of donations, charters, sepulchral monuments, accounts of funerals, or last wills and testaments, as

---

* S. Ambr. ep. 39, ad Faustin. t. 2, p. 944, ed Ben.
† "Da requiem perfectam servo tuo Theodosio, requiem illam quam præparasti sanctis tuis." n. 36, t. 2, p. 1207, ed. Ben.
‡ "Dilexi, et ideo prosequor illum usque ad regionem vivorum; nec deseram donec fletu et precibus inducam virum quo sua merita vocant, in montem Domini sanctum." ib. n. 37, p. 1208. See also his funeral oration on Valentinian, p. 1193, t. 2.
§ S. Ambr. de Obitu Theodosii, n. 3, p. 1197, t. 2.
¶ See Gavant, Comm. in Missal. par. 4, tit. 18, p. 275. Mention is made of these days, after the person's death, by the Apost. Constit. l. 8, c. 42. Palladius in Lausiac. c. 26, &c. See on them Cotelier, not. in Constit. Apost. ib. and especially Dom. Menard. in Concor. Regular, and in Sacram. S. Greg.
** Dial. l. 4, c. 55, t. 2, p. 466.
†† See their lives.

high as any extant, from the time of Constantine the Great, especially from the sixth and seventh ages downwards,[*] mention is usually made of prayer for the dead. In the great provincial council of all the bishops subject to the metropolitical see of Canterbury, held at Cealchythe, or Celchythe, by archbishop Wulfred, in presence of Kenulf, king of Mercia, with his princes and great officers in 816, it was enacted:[†] "As soon as a bishop is dead, let prayers and alms forthwith be offered. At the sounding of a signal in every church throughout our parishes[‡] let every congregation of the servants of God meet at the basilic, and there sing thirty psalms together, for the soul of the deceased. Afterwards let every prelate and abbot sing six hundred psalms, and cause one hundred and twenty masses to be celebrated, and set at liberty three slaves, and give three shillings to every one of them; and let all the servants of God fast one day. And for thirty days after the canonical hours are finished in the assembly, let seven Belts of Pater Nosters[§] also be sung for him. And when this is done let the Obit be renewed on the thirtieth day (*i.e.* dirge and mass sung with the utmost solemnity.) And let them act with as much fidelity in this respect in all churches as they do by custom for the faithful of their own family, by praying for them, that by the favor of common intercession, they may deserve to receive the eternal kingdom,

* See Fontanini, De Vindiciis Veterum Codicum; Miræus, Donat. Belg. and other Diplomatics, &c.
† C. 10, ap. Spelman, Conc. Brit. vol. 1, p. 327, Johnson's English Eccl. Laws and Canons, vol. 1, ad an. 816, Conc. Labbe, t. 7, p. 1489.
‡ The first signals used in churches were a board or iron plate with holes, to be knocked with a hammer, &c., which is retained still among the Greeks, and in the latter part of Holy Week among the Latins. Bells were used in England before this time, (as appears from Bede, Hist. l. 4, c. 23, ad an. 680,) but not universally
§ *Beltidum Pater Noster.* Belts of prayers mean, a certain number of studs fastened in belts or girdles like the strings of beads that are now in use. See Sir Henry Spelman's Glossary, v. Beltis ed. novissimæ.

which is common to all the saints." What was here ordered for bishops was customary in each family for their
own friends, sacrifices being continued for thirty days:
doles distributed, which were alms for the repose of the
departed soul; and beadsmen and beadswomen for alms
received were obliged to say the beads daily at the tomb of
the deceased person: monuments of which are found on
many ancient grave-stones, and in the old writings of all
our churches, where such things have escaped the injuries
of the times. St. Odilo, abbot of Cluni, in 998, instituted
the Commemoration of all the faithful departed in all the
monasteries of his Congregation, on the 1st of November;
which was soon adopted by the whole western church.
The council of Oxford, in 1222, declared it a holiday of the
second class, on which certain necessary and important
kinds of work were allowed. Some dioceses kept it a holiday of precept till noon: only those of Vienne and Tours
and the order of Cluni the whole day: in most places it is
only a day of devotion.* The Greeks have long kept on
Saturday sevennight before Lent, and on Saturday before
Whitsunday, the solemn commemoration of all the faithful departed; but offer up mass every Saturday for them.†

It is certainly a *holy and wholesome thought to pray
for the dead.*‡ Holy and pious because most acceptable to
God, to whom no sacrifices are more honorable and pleasing than those of charity and mercy, especially spiritual,

---

* The Dies Iræ is ascribed by Bzovius (ad an. 1294,) to cardinal Ursini
or Frangipani: by others to Humbert, fifth general of the Dominicans,
&c. The true author was probably some contemplative who desired
to be unknown to the world. Mr. Crashaw, says Wharton, (Essay on
Pope, p. 87,) has translated this piece very well, with a true poetical ge-
nius and fire; to which translation Lord Roscommon is much indebted,
in his admired poem On the Day of Judgment.
† Leo Allat. de Dom. p. 1462. Thomassin, Tr. des Fêtes, et Bened.
XIV. De Festis SS. in Diœcesi Bononiensi.
‡ 2 Mach. xii. 60.

FR. ALBAN BUTLER

and when offered to persons most dear to him. The suffering souls in purgatory are the chosen heirs of heaven, the eternal possession of which kingdom is secured to them, and their names are now written there amongst its glorious princes. God most tenderly loves them, declares them his spouses, enriches them with the precious gifts and ornaments of his grace, and desires to shower down upon them the torrents of his delights, and disclose to them the light of his glory. Only his justice opposes and obliges him to detain them in this distant banishment, and in this place of torments till their debts are discharged to the last farthing. Such is his hatred of the least sin, and such is the opposition which the stain of sin bears to his infinite justice and sanctity. Yet his tender mercy recommends them to the charitable succours which we, as their fellow-members in Christ, have in our power to afford them, and he invites us to appease his anger by interposing our prayers in order to avert them from the weight of his justice. If a compassionate charity towards all that are in any distress, even towards the most flagitious, and those who only labor under temporal miseries and necessities, be a most essential ingredient of a Christian spirit; and that in which the very soul of religion and piety towards God consists: if the least alms given to the poor be highly rewarded by him, will he not exceedingly recompense our charity to his friends and most beloved children, in their extreme necessity? All works of mercy draw down his most abundant graces, and will be richly repaid by Him, who at the last day will adjudge the immortal crowns of his glory to this virtue. But except the leading others to God by our instructions and prayers, what charity, what mercy can we exercise equal to this of succoring the souls in purgatory? A charity not less wholesome and profitable both to them and to ourselves, than pious in itself, and honorable to God. If we consider who they are, and what they suffer, we shall want no other motives to excite us to fervor in it. They are all of them our fellow-members in Jesus Christ. We are united with them by the bands of sincere charity, and by the communion of saints. Every one of them is that brother whom we are bound to love as ourselves. The members of one and the same body conspire mutually to assist one another, as the apostle puts us in mind; so that if one of these members suffers, the others suffer with it; and if one be in honor, the others rejoice with it. If our foot be pricked with a thorn, the whole body suffers with it, and all the other members set themselves at work to relieve it. So ought we in our mystical body. It would be impious and cruel to see a brother in the flames, and not to give him a hand, or afford him some refreshment if we can do it. The dignity of these souls more strongly recommends them to our compassion, and at the same time to our veneration. Though they lie at present at a distance from God, buried in frightful dungeons, under waves of fire, they belong to the happy number of the elect. They are united to God by his grace; they love him above all things, and amidst their torments never cease to bless and praise him, adoring the severity of his justice with perfect resignation and love.

These of whom we speak are not damned souls, enemies of God, separated or alienated from him: but illustrious conquerors of the devil, the world, and hell; holy spirits laded with merits and graces, and bearing the precious badge of their dignity and honor by the nuptial robe of the Lamb with which by an indefeasible right they are clothed. They are the sons of God, heirs of his glory and saints. Yet they are now in a state of suffering, and endure greater torments, than it is possible for any one to suffer, or for our

143

imagination to represent to itself, in this mortal life. They suffer the privation of God, says the council of Florence, the most dreadful of all torments. No tongue can express what a cruel pain this is to a soul separated from the body, impetuously desiring to attain to God, her centre. She seems just enjoying him, attracted by his infinite charms, and carried towards him by a strong innate bent not to be conceived; yet is violently repelled and held back. Whence the poor soul suffers an incomprehensible agony and torment. It is also the opinion of St. Austin and other learned fathers, founded in the words of St. Paul, and the traditionary authority of eminent prelates of the first ages, that they also suffer a material fire like that of hell, which, being created merely for an instrument of the divine vengeance, and blown up by the anger of God, with the most piercing activity torments even spirits not clothed with bodies, as our souls in this life feel the pain of the corporeal senses by the natural law of their union with our bodies. Though it be no article of faith, that the fire here spoken of is not metaphorical, to express the sharpness of these torments, yet that it is real and material is the most probable opinion, grounded in the most venerable authority. "The same fire torments the damned in hell and the just in purgatory," says St. Thomas;[*] who adds:[†] "The least pain in purgatory exceeds the greatest in this life." St. Austin speaks to this point as follows:[‡] "It is said, *He will be saved, as it were, by fire.* Because it is said, *He will be saved,* that fire is contemned. Yet it will be more grievous than whatever a man can suffer in this life. You know how much wicked men have suffered here, and can suffer. Good men may

---

[*] S. Tho. Suppl. qu. 100, a. 2.
[†] Ib. n. 3.
[‡] S. Aug. in Ps. 37, t. 4, p. 295.

undergo as much; and what did any malefactor ever endure which martyrs have not suffered for Christ? All these torments are much more tolerable. Yet see how men do all things rather than suffer them. How much more reason have they to do what God commands them, that they may escape his torments!" Venerable Bede says, "Purgatory fire will be more intolerable than all the torments that can be felt or conceived in this life." Which words are but a repetition of what St. Cæsarius of Arles had written before to this purpose.* "A person," says he, "may say, I am not much concerned how long I remain in purgatory, provided I may come to eternal life. Let no one reason thus. Purgatory fire will be more dreadful than whatever torments can be seen, imagined, or endured in this world. And how does any one know whether he will stay days, months, or years? He who is afraid now to put his finger into the fire, does he not fear lest he be then all buried in torments for a long time?" Do we think that God can find torments in nature sufficient to satisfy his provoked vengeance? No, no. He creates new instruments more violent, pains utterly inconceivable to us.† A soul for one venial sin shall suffer more than all the pains of distempers, the most violent colics, gout, and stone joined in complication; more than all the most cruel torments undergone by malefactors, or invented by the most barbarous tyrants: more than all the tortures of the martyrs summed up together. This is the idea which the fathers give us of purgatory. And how long many souls may have to suffer there we know not.

The church approves perpetual anniversaries for the dead; for some souls may be detained in pains to the end of the world, though after the day of judgment no third state

---

* S. Cæsar. Hom. 1, p. 5, vel in app. Op. S. Aug. t. 5.
† See Bourdaloue, Loriot, Le Rue, &c.

will any longer subsist: God may at the end of the world make the torments of souls which have not then satisfied his justice so intense in one moment that their debts may be discharged. For we know that he will exact a satisfaction to the last farthing. How inexorable was he in punishing his most faithful servant Moses for one small offence!* How inflexible with regard to David† and other penitents! nay, in the person of his own divine Son!‡ This, even in the days of his mercy; but, after death, his justice is all rigor and severity, and can no longer be mitigated by patience. A circumstance which ought particularly to excite our compassion for these suffering souls is, that these holy and illustrious prisoners and debtors to the divine justice, being no longer in the state of meriting, are not able in the least to assist themselves. A sick man afflicted in all his limbs, and a beggar in the most painful and destitute condition, has a tongue left to ask relief; the very sight of his sufferings cannot fail exciting others to pity, comfort, and succor him. At least he can implore heaven: it is never deaf to his prayers. But these souls have no resource but that of patience, resignation, and hope. God answers their moans, that his justice must be satisfied to the last farthing, and that their *night is come in which no man can work.*§ But they address themselves to us, and not having a voice to be heard, they borrow that of the church and its preachers, who, to express their moans, and excite our compassion, cry out to us for them in the words of Job: *Have pity upon me, have pity upon me, at least you my friends; for the hand of God hath smitten me.*¶ Gerson, the pious and learned chancellor of

* Deut. iii. 24, 25.
† 2 Kings (Samuel) xxiv. 15.
‡ Matt. xxvi. 36.
§ John ix. 4.
¶ Job xix. 21.

Paris, represents them crying out to us as follows:[*] "Pray
for us, because we are unable to help ourselves. You who
can do it, lend us your assistance. You who have known
us on earth, you who have loved us, will you now forget
and neglect us? It is commonly said, that a friend is tried
in the day of need. What necessity can be equal to ours?
Let it move your compassion. *A hard heart shall fare ill
at the last day.*[†] Be moved by your own advantage," &c.

Did we behold those dungeons open under our feet,
or had we a view of the torments which these souls endure, how would this spectacle affect us! How would their
pains alone speak to us more pathetically than any words!
How would our eyes stream with tears, and our bowels
be moved, to behold innumerable holy and illustrious
servants of God, and our brethren in Christ, suffering "by
wonderful, but real ways,"[‡] more than our imagination can
represent to itself! Here perhaps lies a parent, a brother, a
bosom-friend and companion. For if we may be permitted
to dive into the secrets of the divine judgments, we shall
be persuaded that the number is very small of those that
departing this life pass immediately to glory without having some satisfaction to make, some debt to cancel. Who
can flatter himself that his soul is so pure before God, as to
have no unperceived irregular attachment or affection, no
stain which he has not perfectly washed away? How rare
is the grace for a soul to leave this infected region without
the least spot! the judgments of God are hidden and unsearchable: but their very inscrutability makes us tremble.
For we know that he will judge justice, and wo even to the
commendable life of man if it be discussed according to the

* Gerson, t. 3, p. 193.
† Ecclus. iii. 26.
‡ S. Aug. de Civ. l. xxi.

rigor of justice, as St. Austin says. Does not St. Peter assure us, that the just man himself will scarce be saved? If then we have lost any dear friends in Christ, while we confide in his mercy, and rejoice in their passage from the region of death to that of life, light, and eternal joy, we have reason to fear some lesser stains may retard their bliss. In this uncertainty why do not we earnestly recommend them to the divine clemency Why do not we say with St. Ambrose in his funeral discourse on Valentinian the Younger, who was murdered in 392, at twenty years of age, while a Catechumen:[*] "Give the holy mysteries to the dead. Let us, with pious earnestness, beg repose for his soul. Lift up your hands with me, O people, that at least by this duty we may make some return for his benefits." Afterwards joining with this emperor his brother Gratian, who was dead before him in 383, he says:[†] "Both blessed, if my prayers can be of any force! No duty shall pass you over in silence: no prayer of mine shall ever be closed without remembering you. No night shall pass you over without some vows of my supplications. You shall have a share in all my sacrifices. If I forget you let my own right hand be forgotten." With the like earnestness this father offered the holy sacrifice for his brother Satyrus.[‡] Perhaps the souls of some dear friends may be suffering on our account; perhaps for their fondness for us, or for sins of which we were the occasion by scandal, provocation, or otherwise; in which cases motives not only of charity, but also of justice call upon us to endeavour to procure them all the relief in our power.

If other motives have less weight with us, we certainly cannot be insensible to that of our own interest. What a

---

[*] S. Ambr. de Obitu Valent. n. 56, t. 2, p. 1189, ed. Bened.
[†] Ib. n. 78, p. 1194.
[‡] De excessu fratris Satyri, n. 80, p. 1135.

comfort shall we find to eternity in the happy company of souls whose enjoyment of bliss we shall have contributed to hasten! What an honor to have ever been able to serve so holy and glorious saints! With what gratitude and earnestness will they repay the favor by their supplications for us, while we still labor amidst the dangers and conflicts of this world! When Joseph foretold Pharaoh's chief butler the recovery of his dignity, he said to him: *Remember me, when it shall be well with thee, and mention me to Pharaoh, that he may bring me out of this place.*[*] Yet he remembered not Joseph, but forgot his fellow-sufferer and benefactor. Not so these pious souls, as St. Bernard observes:[†] only the wicked and depraved, who are strangers to all feelings of virtue, can be ungrateful. This vice is far from the breasts of saints, who are all goodness and charity. Souls delivered and brought to glory by our endeavors will amply repay our kindness by obtaining divine graces for us. God himself will be inclined by our charity to show us also mercy, and to shower down upon us his most precious favors. *Blessed are the merciful, for they shall obtain mercy.*[‡] By having shown this mercy to the suffering souls in purgatory, we shall be particularly entitled to be treated with mercy at our departure hence, and to share more abundantly in the general suffrages of the church, continually offered for all that have slept in Christ. The principal means by which we obtain relief for the suffering souls in purgatory are sacrifice, prayer, and almsdeeds. The unbloody sacrifice has always been offered for the faithful departed no less than for the living.[§] "It was not

[*] Gen. xl. 14.
[†] Serm. 5, in Fest. Omn. Sanct. n. 11.
[‡] Matt. v. 7.
[§] See Card. Bona, Liturg. l. 2, c. 14. Le Brun, sur les Liturgies des quartres premiers siècles, t. 2, pp. 40, 41, 330, 364, 408, &c.

in vain," says St. Chrysostom,* "that the apostles ordained a commemoration of the deceased in the holy and tremendous mysteries. They were sensible of the benefit and advantage which accrues to them from this practice. For, when the congregation stands with open arms as well as the priests, and the tremendous sacrifice is before them, how should our prayers for them not appease God? But this is said of such as have departed in faith."

---

* Hom. 3, in Phil. t. 11, p. 217, ed. Montfauc.